John Paul II:
Essays on Religious Freedom

A 1984 publication of the
Catholic League for Religious and Civil Rights,
1100 West Wells Street · Milwaukee, Wisconsin 53233

Reprinted with permission of *L'Osservatore Romano*,
weekly edition in English.

Table of Contents

FOREWORD

by Virgil C. Blum, S.J.*

Since his election to the Papacy, Pope John Paul II has become one of the most articulate exponents of religious freedom rights in the world. As one charged with the responsibility to promulgate to our modern world God's Word as it pertains to the complexity of our age, he has constantly chosen as one of his major themes the primary necessity of religious freedom, and the responsibility of world leaders to assure religious freedom for each person of the world community. This appeal has transcended doctrinal and political divisions, and has been met with enthusiastic and respectful accord. Hearts have been touched and in many cases public policies affected for the better through his words and his example.

This volume is presented as a testimony to the message of Pope John Paul II. The themes presented here are both universal and timeless, and the editors hope that wider distribution of the Pope's message may alert more readers, Catholic or not, to the God-given right to religious expression for every member of the world community, and the responsibility incumbent on all of us to work vigorously for the preservation and protection of this right.

It is especially fitting that this volume appear under the auspices of the Catholic League for Religious and Civil Rights. Since 1973, this organization has dedicated itself to the mission of educating men and women to their religious freedom rights, and the necessity to labor for their full realization. Through its publications, its educational programs, and its court litigation, the staff of the Catholic League has taken its message of freedom into the American marketplace of ideas. In so doing, the Catholic League has also focused a spotlight on the ugliness of religious prejudice and intolerance which all too often still limit religious freedom, and the League has urged that such prejudice be eradicated from the national soul. Its message has not been universally appreciated. Some have failed to see the need for the vigilance it urges; others have been content to leave the work of preserving our religious freedoms to others; still others have fought mightily that such ideas and practical action not gain

---

*Rev. Virgil C. Blum, S.J., is founder and president of the Catholic League for Religious and Civil Rights and professor emeritus of political science at Marquette University.

currency lest the pervading Secularism of our age and our society be compromised. Despite these obstacles, the Catholic League has continued its work for the Church and American society, and so becomes an example of the type of dedicated effort urged by Pope John Paul II in these pages.

Pope John XXIII in his monumental letter, *Pacem in Terris,* placed the basis for all human rights in the essential dignity of each and every human person. Because the human person possesses this unique and inescapable dignity, such a person "is a subject of rights and duties which immediately and simultaneously flow from his very nature: rights and duties which are therefore universal, inviolable, inalienable" (cf. *Pacem in Terris,* no. 158).

Pope John Paul II, following this fundamental principle, makes unmistakably clear that the human person has an inherent dignity which can never be lost or abdicated. This dignity has its ultimate source in the relationship between God and each human person, and, therefore, religious freedom which protects and encourages this ongoing relationship between each human being and the Creator is the basis and foundation of all other freedoms to which the human person is called and is privileged to possess (cf. Address to the Fifth International Colloquium of Juridical Studies, March 10, 1984, para. 5). Because religious freedom is the foundation for all other freedoms, it is incumbent on each human being to respect the religious convictions of others and to avoid any direct or indirect violation of this relationship with God.

However, this responsibility is not only the exclusive function of individuals in their relationship with each other; legitimate civil authority also is bound to respect this right and to govern in such a way that religious freedom is not compromised. In the words of Pope John Paul II, "The free exercise of religion benefits both individuals and governments. Therefore the obligation to respect religious freedom falls on everyone, both private citizens and legitimate civil authority" (Message to the Secretary-General of the United Nations Organization, December 2, 1978).

The Pope is very clear as to the nature of political activity and the roots of all legitimate civil authority. "All political activity, whether national or international, comes from man, is exercised by man and is for man" (Address to the United Nations, New York, October 2, 1979, para. 6). Since all civil authority rests upon the responsibility to work for the best interests of the human person, it is intolerable, indeed a contradiction, that any civil authority deny or ignore the religious freedom of its citizens.

Yet in the world community and, indeed, in the United States there are those who would deny this principle. In the words of the Pope: "Justice, wisdom and realism all demand that the baneful positions of Secularism be overcome, particularly the erroneous reduction of religion to the purely private sphere" (Message to the Secretary-General of the United Nations, December 2, 1978). Accordingly, religious freedom cannot be taken for granted nor assumed to be secure. Rather, through energetic activity public policy must be influenced and shaped to assure that religious freedom be honored for all citizens. This responsibility is no less incumbent upon the United States than upon any other nation or culture. The pervading Secularism of our society is a continuing threat to our religious freedom: it must be recognized as such and resisted with every bit of energy at our disposal.

The Pope's message in this volume speaks to very specific areas of our human life which demand attention. Marriage and the family, the role of the laity, family life, the right to life of the unborn child, freedom of conscience, our responsibility to the elderly, and the right of parents to direct their children's education all are treated in careful detail. With sensitivity and concern the Pope speaks out on the very issues which so trouble our planet and our American society. His message is forthright and clear. His challenge speaks to the very heart of the human person and the very foundation of human society.

We speak much of peace. The blueprint for peace resides in these pages. May many more of us accept the vision expressed here that the hope of peace, the desire for peace, become reality both for ourselves and for generations still to come!

Freedom of Conscience and of Religion

On the eve of the Madrid Conference on European Security and Cooperation, 1 September 1980, His Holiness Pope John Paul II sent a personal letter to the Heads of State of the nations who signed the Helsinki Final Act (1975), enclosing the following document wherein he submits for their consideration and that of their respective Governments an extensive reflection on the value and content of freedom of conscience and of religion with special reference to the implementation of the Final Act.

1. Because of her religious mission, which is universal in nature, the Catholic Church feels deeply committed to assisting today's men and women in advancing the great cause of justice and peace so as to make our world ever more hospitable and human. These are noble ideals to which people eagerly aspire and for which governments carry a special responsibility. At the same time, because of the changing historical and social situation, their coming into effect—in order to be ever more adequately adapted—needs the continued contribution of new reflections and initiatives, the value of which will depend on the extent to which they proceed from multilateral and constructive dialogue.

If one considers the many factors contributing to peace and justice in the world, one is struck by the ever increasing importance, under their particular aspect, of the widespread aspiration that all men and women be guaranteed equal dignity in sharing material goods, in effectively enjoying spiritual goods, and consequently in enjoying the corresponding inalienable rights.

During these last decades the Catholic Church has reflected deeply on the theme of human rights, especially on freedom of conscience and of religion; in so doing, she has been stimulated by the daily life experience of the Church herself and of the faithful of all areas and social groups. The Church would like to submit a few special considerations on this theme to the distinguished Authorities of the Helsinki Final Act's signatory countries, with a view to encouraging a serious examination of the present situation of this liberty so as to ensure that it is effectively guaranteed everywhere. In doing so, the Church feels she is acting in full accord with the joint commitment contained in the Final Act, namely "to promote and encourage the effective exercise of civil, political, economic, social, cultural, and other liberties and rights, all deriving from the dignity inherent in the human person, and essential for his free and integral development"; she thus intends to make use of the criterion acknowledging "the universal importance of human rights and fundamental liberties, the respect of which is an essential factor of peace, justice, and welfare necessary to the development of friendly relationships and cooperation among them and among all States."

2. It is noted with satisfaction that during the last decades the international Community has shown interest in the safeguarding of human rights and fundamental liberties and has carefully concerned itself with respect for freedom of conscience and of religion in well-known documents such as:

a) the UN Universal Declaration on Human Rights of 10 December 1948 (article 18);

b) the International Covenant on Civil and Political Rights approved by the United Nations on 16 December 1966 (article 18);

c) the Final Act of the Conference on European Security and Cooperation, signed on 1 August 1975 ("Questions related to security in Europe, 1, (a). Declaration on the principles governing mutual relationships among participating States: VII. Respect for human rights and fundamental liberties, including freedom of thought, conscience, religion or conviction ").

Furthermore, the Final Act's section on cooperation regarding "contacts among persons" has a paragraph wherein the participating States "confirm that religious cults, and religious institutions and organizations acting within the constitutional framework of a particular State, and their representatives, may, within the field of activity, have contacts among themselves, hold meetings and exchange information."

Moreover, these international documents reflect an ever growing worldwide conviction resulting from a progressive evolution of the question of human rights in the legal doctrine and public opinion of various countries. Thus today most State Constitutions recognize the principle of respect for freedom of conscience and religion in its fundamental formulation as well as the principle of equality among citizens.

On the basis of all the formulations found in the foregoing national and international legal instruments, it is possible to point out the elements providing a framework and dimension suitable for the full exercise of religious freedom.

First, it is clear that the starting-point for acknowledging and respecting that freedom is the dignity of the human person, who experiences the inner and indestructible exigency of acting freely "according to the imperatives of his own conscience" (cf. text of the Final Act under (c) above). On the basis of his personal convictions, man is led to recognize and follow a religious or metaphysical concept involving his whole life with regard to fundamental choices and attitudes. This inner reflection, even if it does not result in an explicit and positive assertion of faith in God, cannot but be respected in the name of the dignity of each one's conscience, whose hidden searching may not be judged by others. Thus, on the one hand, each individual has the right and duty to seek the truth, and, on the other hand, other persons as well as civil society have the corresponding duty to respect the free spiritual development of each person.

This concrete liberty has its foundation in man's very nature, the characteristic of which is to be free, and it continues to exist—as stated in the Second Vatican Council's Declaration—"even in those who do not live up to their obligation of seeking the truth and adhering to it; the exercise of this right is not to be impeded, provided that the just requirements of public order are observed" (*Dignitatis Humanae,* 2).

A second and no less fundamental element is the fact that religious freedom is expressed not only by internal and exclusively individual acts, since human beings think, act and communicate in relationship with others; "professing" and "practising" a religious faith is expressed through a series of visible acts, whether individual or collective, private or public, producing communion with persons of the same faith, and establishing a bond through which the believer belongs to an organic religious community; that bond may have different degrees or intensities according to the nature and the precepts of the faith or conviction one holds.

3. The Catholic Church has synthesized her thinking on this subject in the Second Vatican Council's Declaration, *Dignitatis Humanae,* promulgated on 7 December 1965, a document which places the Apostolic See under a special obligation.

This Declaration had been preceded by Pope John XXIII's Encyclical *Pacem in Terris,* dated 11 April 1963, which solemnly emphasized the fact that everyone has "the right to be able to worship God in accordance with the right dictates of his conscience."

The same Declaration of the Second Vatican Council was then taken up again in various documents of Pope Paul VI, in the 1974 Synod of Bishops' message, and more recently in the message to the United Nations Organization during the papal visit on 2 October 1979, which repeats it essentially: "In accordance with their dignity, all human beings, because they are persons, that is, beings endowed with reason and free will and therefore bearing a personal responsibility, are both impelled by their nature and bound by a moral obligation to seek the truth, especially religious truth. They are also bound to adhere to the truth once they come to know it and to direct their whole lives in accordance with its demands" (*Dignitatis Humanae,* 2). "The practice of religion by its very nature consists primarly of those voluntary and free internal acts by which a human being directly sets his course towards God. No merely human power can either command or prohibit acts of this kind. But man's social nature itself requires that he give external expression to his internal acts of religion, that he communicate with others in religious matters and that he profess his religion in community" (*Dignitatis Humanae,* 3).

"These words," the UN address added, "touch the very substance of the question. They also show how even the confrontation between the religious view and the agnostic or even atheistic view of the world, which is one of the 'signs of the times' of the present age, could preserve honest and respectful human dimensions without violating the essential rights of conscience of any man or woman living on earth" (Address to the 34th General Assembly of the United Nations, no. 20).

On the same occasion, the conviction was expressed that "respect for the dignity of the human person would seem to demand that, when the exact tenor of the exercise of religious freedom is being discussed or determined with a view to national laws or international conventions, the institutions that are by their nature at the service of religion should also be brought in." This is because, when religious freedom is to be given substance, if the participation of those most concerned in it and who have special experience of it and responsibility for it is omitted, there is a danger of setting arbitrary norms of application and of "imposing, in so intimate a field of man's life, rules or restrictions that are opposed to his true religious needs" (Address to the UN 34th General Assembly, no. 20).

4. In the light of the foregoing premises and principles, the Holy See sees it as its right and duty to envisage an analysis of the specific elements corresponding to the concept of "religious freedom" and of which they are the application insofar as they follow from the requirements of individuals and communities, or insofar as they are necessary for enabling them to carry out their concrete activities. In fact, in the expression and practice of religious freedom one notices the presence of closely interrelated individual and community aspects, private and public, so that enjoying religious freedom includes connected and complimentary dimensions:

a) *at the personal level,* the following have to be taken into account:

— freedom to hold or not to hold a particular faith and to join the corresponding confessional community;

— freedom to perform acts of prayer and worship, individually and collectively, in private or in public, and to have churches or places of worship according to the needs of the believers;

— freedom for parents to educate their children in the religious convictions that inspire their own life, and to have them attend catechetical and religious instruction as provided by their faith community;

— freedom for families to choose the schools or other means which provide this sort of education for their children, without having to sustain directly or indirectly extra charges which would in fact deny them this freedom;

— freedom for individuals to receive religious assistance wherever they are, especially in public health institutions (clinics and hospitals), in military establishments, during compulsory public service, and in places of detention;

— freedom, at personal, civic or social levels, from any form of coercion to perform acts contrary to one's faith, or to receive an education or to join groups or associations with principles opposed to one's religious convictions;

— freedom not to be subjected, on religious grounds, to forms of restriction and discrimination, vis-a-vis one's fellow-citizens, in all aspects of life (in all matters concerning one's career, including study, employment or profession; one's participation in civic and social responsibilities, etc.).

b) at the community level, account has to be taken of the fact that religious denominations, in bringing together believers of a given faith, exist and act as social bodies organized according to their own doctrinal principles and institutional purposes.

The Church as such, and confessional communities in general, need to enjoy specific liberties in order to conduct their life and to pursue their purposes; among such liberties the following are to be mentioned especially:

— freedom to have their own internal hierarchy or equivalent ministers freely chosen by the communities according to their constitutional norms;

—freedom for religious authorities (notably, in the Catholic Church, for bishops and other ecclesiastical superiors) to exercise their ministry freely, ordain priests or ministers, appoint to ecclesiastical offices, communicate and have contacts with those belonging to their religious denomination;

—freedom to have their own institutions for religious training and theological studies, where candidates for priesthood and religious consecration can be freely admitted;

—freedom to receive and publish religious books related to faith and worship, and to have free use of them;

—freedom to proclaim and communicate the teaching of the faith, whether by the spoken or the written word, inside as well as outside places of worship, and to make known their moral teaching on human activites and on the organization of society; this being in accordance with the commitment, included in the Helsinki Final Act, to facilitate the spreading of information, of culture, of exchange of knowledge and experiences in the field of education; which corresponds moreover in the religious field to the Church's mission of evangelization;

— freedom to use the media of social communication (press, radio, television) for the same purpose;

— freedom to carry out educational, charitable, and social activities so as to put into practice the religious precept of love for neighbour, particularly for those most in need.

Furthermore:

— With regard to religious communities which, like the Catholic Church, have a supreme Authority responsible at world level (in line with the directives of their faith) for the unity of communion that binds together all pastors and believers in the same confession (a responsibility exercised through magisterium and jurisdiction): freedom to maintain mutual relations of communication between that authority and the local pastors and religious communities; freedom to make known the documents and texts of the magisterium (encyclicals, instructions, etc.);

— at the international level: freedom of free exchange in the field of communication, cooperation, religious solidarity, and more particularly the possibility of holding multinational or international meetings;

— also at the international level, freedom for religious communities to exchange information and other contributions of a theological or religious nature.

5. As was said earlier, freedom of conscience and of religion, including the aforementioned elements, is a primary and inalienable right of the human person; what is more, insofar as it touches the innermost sphere of the spirit, one can even say that it upholds the justification, deeply rooted in each individual, of all other liberties. Of course, such freedom can only be exercised in a responsible way, that is in accordance with ethical principles and by respecting equality and justice, which in turn can be strengthened, as mentioned before, through dialogue with those institutions whose nature is to serve religion.

6. The Catholic Church is not confined to a particular territory and she has no geographical borders; her members are men and women of all regions of the world. She knows, from many centuries of experience,

that suppression, violation or restriction of religious freedom have caused suffering and bitterness, moral and material hardship, and that even today there are millions of people enduring these evils. By contrast, the recognition, guarantee and respect of religious freedom bring serenity to individuals and peace to the social community; they also represent an important factor in strengthening a nation's moral cohesion, in improving people's common welfare, and in enriching the cooperation among nations in an atmosphere of mutual trust.

In addition, the wholesome implementation of the principle of religious freedom will contribute to the formation of citizens who, in full recognition of the moral order, "will be obedient to lawful authority and be lovers of true freedom; people, in other words, who will come to decisions on their own judgment, and, in the light of truth, govern their activities with a sense of responsibility, and strive after what is true and right, willing always to join with others in cooperative effort" (*Dignitatis Humanae,* 8).

Moreover, if it is properly understood, religious freedom will help to ensure the order and common welfare of each nation, of each society, for, when individuals know that their fundamental rights are protected, they are better prepared to work for the common welfare.

Respect for this principle of religious freedom will also contribute to strengthening international peace which, on the contrary, is threatened by any violation of human rights, as pointed out in the aforementioned UN address, and especially by unjust distribution of material goods and violation of the objective rights of the spirit, of human conscience and creativity, including man's relation to God. Only the effective protection of the fullness of rights for every individual without discrimination can guarantee peace down to its very foundations.

7. In this perspective, through the above presentation the Holy See intends to serve the cause of peace, in the hope it may contribute to the improvement of such an important sector of human and social life, and thus of international life also.

It goes without saying that the Apostolic See has no thought or intention of failing to give due respect to the sovereign prerogatives of any State. On the contrary, the Church has a deep concern for the dignity and rights of every nation; she has the desire to contribute to the welfare of each one and she commits herself to do so.

Thus the Holy See wishes to stimulate reflection, so that the civil authorities of the various countries may see to what extent the above considerations deserve thorough examination. If such reflection can lead to recognizing the possibility of improving the present situation, the Holy

See declares itself fully available to open a fruitful dialogue to that end, in a spirit of sincerity and openness.

From the Vatican, 1 September 1980.

Education and the Family

From the Apostolic Exhortation
Familiaris Consortio

The Right and Duty of Parents Regarding Education

36. The task of giving education is rooted in the primary vocation of married couples to participate in God's creative activity: by begetting in love and for love a new person who has within himself or herself the vocation to growth and development, parents by that very fact take on the task of helping that person effectively to live a fully human life. As the Second Vatican Council recalled, "Since parents have conferred life on their children, they have a most solemn obligation to educate their offspring. Hence, parents must be acknowledged as the first and foremost educators of their children. Their role as educators is so decisive that scarcely anything can compensate for their failure in it. For it devolves on parents to create a family atmosphere so animated with love and reverence for God and others that a well-rounded personal and social development will be fostered among the children. Hence, the family is the first school of those social virtues which every society needs" (Declaration on Christian Education, *Gravissimum Educationis,* no. 3).

The right and duty of parents to give education is essential, since it is connected with the transmission of human life; it is *original and primary* with regard to the educational role of others, on account of the uniqueness of the loving relationship between parents and children; and it is *irreplaceable and inalienable,* and therefore incapable of being entirely delegated to others or usurped by others.

In addition to these characteristics, it cannot be forgotten that the most basic element, so basic that it qualifies the educational role of parents, is *parental love,* which finds fulfillment in the task of education as it completes and perfects its service of life: as well as being a *source,* the parents' love is also the *animating principle* and therefore the *norm* inspiring and guiding all concrete educational activity, enriching it with the values of kindness, constancy, goodness, service, disinterestedness and self-sacrifice that are the most precious fruit of love.

37. Even amid the difficulties of the work of education, difficulties which are often greater today, parents must trustingly and courageously train their children in the essential values of human life. Children must

grow up with a correct attitude of freedom with regard to material goods, by adopting a simple and austere life style and being fully convinced that "man is more precious for what he is than for what he has" (Second Vatican Ecumenical Council, Pastoral Constitution on the Church in the Modern World, *Gaudium et Spes,* no. 35).

In a society shaken and split by tensions and conflicts caused by the violent clash of various kinds of individualism and selfishness, children must be enriched not only with a sense of true justice, which alone leads to respect for the personal dignity of each individual, but also and more powerfully by a sense of true love, understood as sincere solicitude and disinterested service with regard to others, especially the poorest and those in most need. The family is the first and fundamental school of social living: as a community of love, it finds in self-giving the law that guides it and makes it grow. The self-giving that inspires the love of husband and wife for each other is the model and norm for the self-giving that must be practiced in the relationships between brothers and sisters and the different generations living together in the family. And the communion and sharing that are part of everyday life in the home at times of joy and at times of difficulty are the most concrete and effective pedagogy for the active, responsible and fruitful inclusion of the children in the wider horizon of society.

Education in love as self-giving is also the indispensable premise for parents called to give their children a clear and delicate *sex education.* Faced with a culture that largely reduces human sexuality to the level of something commonplace, since it interprets and lives it in a reductive and impoverished way by linking it solely with the body and with selfish pleasure, the educational service of parents must aim firmly at a training in the area of sex that is truly and fully personal: for sexuality is an enrichment of the whole person—body, emotions and soul—and it manifests its inmost meaning in leading the person to the gift of self in love.

Sex education, which is a basic right and duty of parents, must always be carried out under their attentive guidance, whether at home or in educational centers chosen and controlled by them. In this regard, the Church reaffirms the law of subsidiarity, which the school is bound to observe when it cooperates in sex education, by entering into the same spirit that animates the parents.

In this context *education for chastity* is absolutely essential, for it is a virtue that develops a person's authentic maturity and makes him or her capable of respecting and fostering the "nuptial meaning" of the body. Indeed Christian parents, discerning the signs of God's call, will devote special attention and care to education in virginity or celibacy as the supreme form of that self-giving that constitutes the very meaning of human sexuality.

In view of the close links between the sexual dimension of the person and his or her ethical values, education must bring the children to a knowledge of and respect for the moral norms as the necessary and highly valuable guarantee for responsible personal growth in human sexuality.

For this reason the Church is firmly opposed to an often widespread form of imparting sex information dissociated from moral principles. That would merely be an introduction to the experience of pleasure and a stimulus leading to the loss of serenity—while still in the years of innocence—by opening the way to vice.

The Mission To Educate and the Sacrament of Marriage

38. For Christian parents the mission to educate, a mission rooted, as we have said, in their participation in God's creating activity, has a new specific source in the sacrament of marriage, which consecrates them for the strictly Christian education of their children: that is to say, it calls upon them to share in the very authority and love of God the Father and Christ the Shepherd, and in the motherly love of the Church, and it enriches them with wisdom, counsel, fortitude and all the other gifts of the Holy Spirit in order to help the children in their growth as human beings and as Christians.

The sacrament of marriage gives to the educational role the dignity and vocation of being really and truly a "ministry" of the Church at the service of the building up of her members. So great and splendid is the educational ministry of Christian parents that Saint Thomas has no hesitation in comparing it with the ministry of priests: "Some only propagate and guard spiritual life by a spiritual ministry: this is the role of the sacrament of Orders; others do this for both corporal and spiritual life, and this is brought about by the sacrament of marriage, by which a man and a woman join in order to beget offspring and bring them up to worship God" (St. Thomas Aquinas, *Summa contra Gentiles,* IV, 58).

A vivid and attentive awareness of the mission that they have received with the sacrament of marriage will help Christian parents to place themselves at the service of their children's education with great serenity and trustfulness, and also with a sense of responsibility before God, who calls them and gives them the mission of building up the Church in their children. Thus in the case of baptized people, the family, called together by word and sacrament as the Church of the home, is both teacher and mother, the same as the worldwide Church.

First Experience of the Church

39. The mission to educate demands that Christian parents should present to their children all the topics that are necessary for the gradual maturing of their personality from a Christian and ecclesial point of view. They will therefore follow the educational lines mentioned above, taking care to show their children the depths of significance to which the faith and love of Jesus Christ can lead. Furthermore, their awareness that the Lord is entrusting to them the growth of a child of God, a brother or sister of Christ, a temple of the Holy Spirit, a member of the Church, will support Christian parents in their task of strengthening the gift of divine grace in their children's souls.

The Second Vatican Council describes the content of Christian education as follows: "Such an education does not merely strive to foster maturity . . . in the human person. Rather, its principal aims are these: that as baptized persons are gradually introduced into a knowledge of the mystery of salvation, they may daily grow more conscious of the gift of faith which they have received; that they may learn to adore God the Father in spirit and in truth (cf. *Jn.* 4:23), especially through liturgical worship; that they may be trained to conduct their personal life in true righteousness and holiness, according to their new nature (*Eph.* 4:22-24), and thus grow to maturity, to the stature of the fullness of Christ (cf. *Eph.* 4:13), and devote themselves to the upbuilding of the Mystical Body. Moreover, aware of their calling, they should grow accustomed to giving witness to the hope that is in them (cf. 1 *Pt.* 3:15), and to promoting the Christian transformation of the world" (Declaration on Christian Education, *Gravissimum Educationis,* no. 2).

The Synod too, taking up and developing the indications of the Council, presented the educational mission of the Christian family as a true ministry through which the Gospel is transmitted and radiated, so that family life itself becomes an itinerary of faith and in some way a Christian initiation and a school of following Christ. Within a family that is aware of this gift, as Paul VI wrote, "all the members evangelize and are evangelized" (Apostolic Exhortation *Evangelii Nuntiandi,* no. 71: *AAS* 68 (1976), 60-61).

By virtue of their ministry of educating, parents are, through the witness of their lives, the first heralds of the Gospel for their children. Furthermore, by praying with their children, by reading the word of God with them and by introducing them deeply through Christian initiation into the Body of Christ—both the Eucharistic and the ecclesial Body—they become fully parents, in that they are begetters not only of bodily life but also of the life that through the Spirit's renewal flows from the Cross and Resurrection of Christ.

In order that Christian parents may worthily carry out their ministry of educating, the Synod Fathers expressed the hope that a suitable *catechism for families* would be prepared, one that would be clear, brief and easily assimilated by all. The Episcopal Conferences were warmly invited to contribute to producing this catechism.

Relations with Other Educating Agents

40. The family is the primary but not the only and exclusive educating community. Man's community aspect itself—both civil and ecclesial—demands and leads to a broader and more articulated activity resulting from well-ordered collaboration between the various agents of education. All these agents are necessary, even though each can and should play its part in accordance with the special competence and contribution proper to itself (cf. Second Vatican Ecumenical Council, Declaration on Christian Education, *Gravissimum Educationis,* no. 3).

The educational role of the Christian family therefore has a very important place in organic pastoral work. This involves a new form of cooperation between parents and Christian communities, and between the various educational groups and pastors. In this sense, the renewal of the Catholic school must give special attention both to the parents of the pupils and to the formation of a perfect educating community.

The right of parents to choose an education in conformity with their religious faith must be absolutely guaranteed.

The State and the Church have the obligation to give families all possible aid to enable them to perform their educational role properly. Therefore both the Church and the State must create and foster the institutions and activities that families justly demand, and the aid must be in proportion to the families' needs. However, those in society who are in charge of schools must never forget that the parents have been appointed by God Himself as the first and principal educators of their children and that their right is completely inalienable.

But corresponding to their right, parents have a serious duty to commit themselves totally to a cordial and active relationship with the teachers and the school authorities.

If ideologies opposed to the Christian faith are taught in the schools, the family must join with other families, if possible through family associations, and with all its strength and with wisdom help the young not to depart from the faith. In this case the family needs special assistance from pastors of souls, who must never forget that parents have the inviolable right to entrust their children to the ecclesial community.

Manifold Service to Life

41. Fruitful married love expresses itself in serving life in many ways. Of these ways, begetting and educating children are the most immediate, specific and irreplaceable. In fact, every act of true love towards a human being bears witness to and perfects the spiritual fecundity of the family, since it is an act of obedience to the deep inner dynamism of love as self-giving to others.

For everyone this perspective is full of value and commitment, and it can be an inspiration in particular for couples who experience physical sterility.

Christian families, recognizing with faith all human beings as children of the same heavenly Father, will respond generously to the children of other families, giving them support and love not as outsiders but as members of the one family of God's children. Christian parents will thus be able to spread their love beyond the bonds of flesh and blood, nourishing the links that are rooted in the spirit and that develop through concrete service to the children of other families, who are often without even the barest necessities.

Christian families will be able to show greater readiness to adopt and foster children who have lost their parents or have been abandoned by them. Rediscovering the warmth of affection of a family, these children will be able to experience God's loving and provident fatherhood witnessed to by Christian parents, and they will thus be able to grow up with serenity and confidence in life. At the same time the whole family will be enriched with the spiritual values of a wider fraternity.

Family fecundity must have an unceasing "creativity," a marvelous fruit of the Spirit of God, who opens the eyes of the heart to discover the new needs and sufferings of our society and gives courage for accepting them and responding to them. A vast field of activity lies open to families: today, even more preoccupying than child abandonment is the phenomenon of social and cultural exclusion, which seriously affects the elderly, the sick, the disabled, drug addicts, ex-prisoners, etc.

This broadens enormously the horizons of the parenthood of Christian families: these and many other urgent needs of our time are a challenge to their spiritually fruitful love. With families and through them, the Lord Jesus continues to "have compassion" on the multitudes.

42. "Since the Creator of all things has established the conjugal partnership as the beginning and basis of human society," the family is "the first and vital cell of society" (Second Vatican Ecumenical Council, Decree on the Apostolate of the Laity, *Apostolicam Actuositatem,* no. 11).

The family has vital and organic links with society, since it is its foundation and nourishes it continually through its role of service to life: it is from the family that citizens come to birth and it is within the family that they find the first school of the social virtues that are the animating principle of the existence and development of society itself.

Thus, far from being closed in on itself, the family is by nature and vocation open to other families and to society, and undertakes its social role.

Family Life as an Experience of Communion and Sharing

43. The very experience of communion and sharing that should characterize the family's daily life represents its first and fundamental contribution to society.

The relationships between the members of the family community are inspired and guided by the law of "free giving." By respecting and fostering personal dignity in each and every one as the only basis for value, this free giving takes the form of heartfelt acceptance, encounter and dialogue, disinterested availability, generous service and deep solidarity.

Thus the fostering of authentic and mature communion between persons within the family is the first and irreplaceable school of social life, and example and stimulus for the broader community relationships marked by respect, justice, dialogue and love.

The family is thus, as the Synod Fathers recalled, the place of origin and the most effective means for humanizing and personalizing society: it makes an original contribution in depth to building up the world, by making possible a life that is properly speaking human, in particular by guarding and transmitting virtues and "values." As the Second Vatican Council states, in the family "the various generations come together and help one another to grow wiser and to harmonize personal rights with the other requirements of social living" (Second Vatican Ecumenical Council, Pastoral Constitution on the Church in the Modern World, *Gaudium et Spes,* no. 52).

Consequently, faced with a society that is running the risk of becoming more and more depersonalized and standardized and therefore inhuman and dehumanizing, with the negative results of many forms of escapism—such as alcoholism, drugs and even terrorism—the family possesses and continues still to release formidable energies capable of taking man out of his anonymity, keeping him conscious of his personal dignity, enriching him with deep humanity and actively placing him, in his uniqueness and unrepeatability, within the fabric of society.

44. The social role of the family certainly cannot stop short at procrea-

tion and education, even if this constitutes its primary and irreplaceable form of expression.

Families therefore, either singly or in association, can and should devote themselves to manifold social service activities, especially in favor of the poor, or at any rate for the benefit of all people and situations that cannot be reached by the public authorities' welfare organization.

The social contribution of the family has an original character of its own, one that should be given greater recognition and more decisive encouragement, especially as the children grow up, and actually involving all its members as much as possible (cf. Second Vatican Ecumenical Council, Decree on the Apostolate of the Laity, *Apostolicam Actuositatem,* no. 11).

In particular, note must be taken of the ever greater importance in our society of hospitality in all its forms, from opening the door of one's home and still more of one's heart to the pleas of one's brothers and sisters, to concrete efforts to ensure that every family has its own home, as the natural environment that preserves it and makes it grow. In a special way the Christian family is called upon to listen to the Apostle's recommendation: "Practice hospitality" (*Rom.* 12:13), and therefore, imitating Christ's example and sharing in His love, to welcome the brother or sister in need: "Whoever gives to one of these little ones even a cup of cold water because he is a disciple, truly, I say to you, he shall not lose his reward" (*Mt.* 10:42).

The social role of families is called upon to find expression also in the form of *political intervention:* families should be the first to take steps to see that the laws and institutions of the State not only do not offend but support and positively defend the rights and duties of the family. Along these lines, families should grow in awareness of being "protagonists" of what is known as "family politics" and assume responsibility for transforming society; otherwise families will be the first victims of the evils that they have done no more than note with indifference. The Second Vatican Council's appeal to go beyond an individualistic ethic therefore also holds good for the family as such (cf. Second Vatican Ecumenical Council, Pastoral Constitution on the Church in the Modern World, *Gaudium et Spes,* no. 30).

Society at the Service of the Family

45. Just as the intimate connection between the family and society demands that the family be open to and participate in society and its development, so also it requires that society should never fail in its fundamental task of respecting and fostering the family.

The family and society have complementary functions in defending and fostering the good of each and every human being. But society—more specifically the State—must recognize that "the family is a society in its own original right" (Second Vatican Ecumenical Council, Declaration on Religious Freedom, *Dignitatis Humanae,* no. 5) and so society is under a grave obligation in its relations with the family to adhere to the principle of subsidiarity.

By virtue of this principle, the State cannot and must not take away from families the functions that they can just as well perform on their own or in free associations; instead it must positively favor and encourage as far as possible responsible initiative by families. In the conviction that the good of the family is an indispensable and essential value of the civil community, the public authorities must do everything possible to ensure that families have all those aids—economic, social, educational, political and cultural assistance—that they need in order to face all their responsibilities in a human way.

The Charter of Family Rights

46. The ideal of mutual support and development between the family and society is often very seriously in conflict with the reality of their separation and even opposition.

In fact, as was repeatedly denounced by the Synod, the situation experienced by many families in various countries is highly problematical, if not entirely negative: institutions and laws unjustly ignore the inviolable rights of the family and of the human person; and society, far from putting itself at the service of the family, attacks it violently in its values and fundamental requirements. Thus the family, which in God's plan is the basic cell of society and a subject of rights and duties before the State or any other community, finds itself the victim of society, of the delays and slowness with which it acts, and even of its blatant injustice.

For this reason, the Church openly and strongly defends the rights of the family against the intolerable usurpations of society and the State. In particular, the Synod Fathers mentioned the following rights of the family:

— the right to exist and progress as a family, that is to say, the right of every human being, even if he or she is poor, to found a family and to have adequate means to support it;

— the right to exercise its responsibility regarding the transmission of life and to educate children;

— the right to the intimacy of conjugal and family life;

— the right to the stability of the bond and of the institution of marriage;

— the right to believe in and profess one's faith and to propagate it;

— the right to bring up children in accordance with the family's own traditions and religious and cultural values, with the necessary instruments, means and institutions;

— the right, especially of the poor and the sick, to obtain physical, social, political and economic security;

— the right to housing suitable for living family life in a proper way;

— the right to expression and to representation, either directly or through associations, before the economic, social and cultural public authorities and lower authorities;

— the right to form associations with other families and institutions, in order to fulfill the family's role suitably and expeditiously;

— the right to protect minors by adequate institutions and legislation from harmful drugs, pornography, alcoholism, etc.;

— the right to wholesome recreation of a kind that also fosters family values;

— the right of the elderly to a worthy life and a worthy death;

— the right to emigrate as a family in search of a better life (cf. *Propositio* 42).

Acceding to the Synod's explicit request, the Holy See will give prompt attention to studying these suggestions in depth and to the preparation of a Charter of Rights of the Family, to be presented to the quarters and authorities concerned.

The Christian Family's Grace and Responsibility

47. The social role that belongs to every family pertains by a new and original right to the Christian family, which is based on the sacrament of marriage. By taking up the human reality of the love between husband and wife in all its implications, the sacrament gives to Christian couples and parents a power and a commitment to live their vocation as lay people and therefore to "seek the kingdom of God by engaging in temporal affairs and by ordering them according to the plan of God" (Second Vatican Ecumenical Council, Dogmatic Constitution on the Church, *Lumen Gentium,* no. 31).

The social and political role is included in the kingly mission of service in which Christian couples share by virtue of the sacrament of marriage, and they receive both a command which they cannot ignore and a grace which sustains and stimulates them.

The Christian family is thus called upon to offer everyone a witness of generous and disinterested dedication to social matters, through a "preferential option" for the poor and disadvantaged. Therefore, advancing in its following of the Lord by special love for all the poor, it must have special concern for the hungry, the poor, the old, the sick, drug victims and those who have no family.

For a New International Order

48. In view of the worldwide dimension of various social questions nowadays, the family has seen its role with regard to the development of society extended in a completely new way: it now also involves cooperating for a new international order, since it is only in worldwide solidarity that the enormous and dramatic issues of world justice, the freedom of peoples and the peace of humanity can be dealt with and solved.

The spiritual communion between Christian families, rooted in a common faith and hope and given life by love, constitutes an inner energy that generates, spreads and develops justice, reconciliation, fraternity and peace among human beings. Insofar as it is a "small-scale Church," the Christian family is called upon, like the "large-scale Church," to be a sign of unity for the world and in this way to exercise its prophetic role by bearing witness to the Kingdom and peace of Christ, towards which the whole world is journeying.

Christian families can do this through their educational activity—that is to say by presenting to their children a model of life based on the values of truth, freedom, justice and love—both through active and responsible involvement in the authentically human growth of society and its institutions, and by supporting in various ways the associations specifically devoted to international issues.

The Sanctity of Human Life

Following is the text of Pope John Paul II's homily at the Mass on the Washington, D.C. Mall, October 7, 1979.

Dear brothers and sisters in Jesus Christ: In His dialogue with His listeners, Jesus was faced one day with an attempt by some Pharisees to get Him to endorse their current views regarding the nature of marriage.

Jesus answered by reaffirming the teaching of scripture: "At the beginning of creation God made them male and female; for this reason a man shall leave his father and mother and the two shall become one. They are no longer two but one in flesh. Therefore let no man separate what God has joined."

The Gospel according to Mark immediately adds the description of a scene with which we are all familiar.

This scene shows Jesus becoming indignant when He noticed how His own disciples tried to prevent the people from bringing their children closer to Him.

And so He said: "Let the children come to me and do not hinder them. It is to just such as these that the Kingdom of God belongs. Then he embraced them and blessed them, placing his hands on them."

In proposing these readings, today's liturgy invites all of us to reflect on the nature of marriage, on the family and on the value of life—three themes that are so closely interconnected.

I shall all the more gladly lead you in reflecting on the word of God as proposed by the church today, because all over the world the bishops are discussing marriage and family life as they are lived in all dioceses and nations.

The bishops are doing this in preparation for the next World Synod of Bishops, which has as its theme: "The Role of the Christian Family in the Contemporary World."

Your own bishops have designated next year as a year of study, planning and pastoral review with regard to the family.

For a variety of reasons there is a renewed interest throughout the world in marriage, in family life, and in the value of all human life.

This very Sunday marks the beginning of the annual Respect Life program, through which the church in the United States intends to reiterate its conviction regarding the inviolability of human life in all stages.

Let us then, all together, renew our esteem for the value of human life, remembering also that, through Christ, all human life has been redeemed.

I do not hesitate to proclaim before you and before the world that all human life—from the moment of conception and through all subsequent stages—is sacred, because human life is created in the image and likeness of God.

Nothing surpasses the greatness or dignity of a human person.

Human life is not just an idea or an abstraction; human life is the concrete reality of a being that lives, that acts, that grows and develops; human life is the concrete reality of a being that is capable of love, and of service to humanity.

Let me repeat what I told the people during my recent pilgrimage to my homeland: "If a person's right to life is violated at the moment in which he is first conceived in his mother's womb, an indirect blow is struck also at the whole of the moral order, which serves to ensure the inviolable goods of man.

"Among those goods, life occupies the first place.

"The church defends the right to life, not only in regard to the majesty of the Creator, Who is the first giver of this life, but also in respect of the essential good of the human person."

Human life is precious because it is the gift of a God Whose love is infinite, and when God gives life, it is forever.

Life is also precious because it is the expression and the fruit of love.

This is why life should spring up within the setting of marriage, and why marriage and the parents' love for one another should be marked by generosity in self-giving.

The great danger for family life, in the midst of any society whose idols are pleasure, comfort and independence, lies in the fact that people close their hearts and become selfish.

The fear of making permanent commitments can change the mutual love of husband and wife into two loves of self—two loves existing side by side, until they end in separation.

In the sacrament of marriage, a man and a woman—who at baptism became members of Christ and hence have the duty of manifesting Christ's attitude in their lives—are assured of the help they need to develop their love in a faithful and indissoluble union, and to respond with generosity to the gift of parenthood.

As the Second Vatican Council declared: "Through this sacrament, Christ Himself becomes present in the life of the married couple and accompanies them, so that they may love each other and their children, just as Christ loved His church by giving Himself up for her."

In order that Christian marriage may favor the total good and development of the married couple, it must be inspired by the Gospel, and thus be open to new life—new life to be given and accepted generously.

The couple is also called to create a family atmosphere in which children can be happy, and lead full and worthy human and Christian lives.

To maintain a joyful family requires much from both the parents and the children.

Each member of the family has to become, in a special way, the servant of the others and share their burdens.

Each one must show concern, not only for his or her own life, but also for the lives of the other members of the family: their needs, their hopes, their ideals.

Decisions about the number of children and the sacrifices to be made for them must not be taken only with a view to adding to comfort and preserving a peaceful existence.

Reflecting upon this matter before God, with the grace drawn from the sacrament, and guided by the teaching of the church, parents will remind themselves that it is certainly less serious to deny their children certain comforts or material advantages than to deprive them of the presence of brothers and sisters, who could help them to grow in humanity and to realize the beauty of life at all its ages and in all its variety.

If parents fully realized the demands and the opportunities that this great sacrament brings, they could not fail to join in Mary's hymn to the author of life—to God—Who has made them His chosen fellow-workers.

All human beings ought to value every person for his or her uniqueness as a creature of God, called to be a brother or sister of Christ by reason of the incarnation and the universal redemption.

For us, the sacredness of human life is based on these premises.

And it is on these same premises that there is based our celebration of life—all human life.

This explains our efforts to defend human life against every influence or action that threatens or weakens it, as well as our endeavors to make every life more human in all its aspects.

And so, we will stand up every time that human life is threatened.

When the sacredness of life before birth is attacked, we will stand up and proclaim that no one ever has the authority to destroy unborn life.

When a child is described as a burden or is looked upon only as a means to satisfy an emotional need, we will stand up and insist that every child is a unique and unrepeatable gift of God, with the right to a loving and united family.

When the institution of marriage is abandoned to human selfishness or reduced to a temporary, conditional arrangement that can easily be terminated, we will stand up and affirm the indissolubility of the marriage bond.

When the value of the family is threatened because of social and economic pressures, we will stand up and reaffirm that the family is "necessary not only for the private good of every person, but also for the common good of every society, nation and state."

When freedom is used to dominate the weak, to squander natural resources and energy, and to deny basic necessities to people, we will stand up and reaffirm the demands of justice and social love.

When the sick, the aged or the dying are abandoned in loneliness, we will stand up and proclaim that they are worthy of love, care and respect.

I make my own the words which Paul VI spoke last year to the American bishops:

"We are convinced, moreover, that all efforts made to safeguard human rights actually benefit life itself. Everything aimed at banishing discrimination—in law or in fact—which is based on race, origin, color, culture, sex or religion is a service to life.

"When the rights of minorities are fostered, when the mentally or physically handicapped are assisted, when those on the margin of society are given a voice—in all these instances the dignity of life, and the sacredness of human life, are furthered.

"In particular, every contribution made to better the moral climate of society, to oppose permissiveness and hedonism, and all assistance to the family, which is the source of new life, effectively uphold the values of life."

Much remains to be done to support those whose lives are wounded and to restore hope to those who are afraid of life.

Courage is needed to resist pressures and false slogans, to proclaim the supreme dignity of all life, and to demand that society itself give it its protection.

A distinguished American, Thomas Jefferson, once stated: "The care of human life and happiness and not their destruction is the just and only legitimate object of good government."

I wish therefore to praise all the members of the Catholic Church and other Christian churches, all men and women of the Judeo-Christian heritage, as well as all people of good will who unite in common dedication for the defense of life in its fullness and for the promotion of all human rights.

Our celebration of life forms part of the celebration of the Eucharist.

Our Lord and Savior, through His death and Resurrection, has become for us the bread of life and the pledge of eternal life.

In Him we find the courage, perseverance and inventiveness which we need in order to promote and defend life within our families and throughout the world.

Dear brothers and sisters: We are confident that Mary, the mother of God and the mother of life, will give us her help so that our way of living will always reflect our admiration and gratitude for God's gift of love that is life.

We know that she, mother of God and mother of life, will help us to use every day that is given to us as an opportunity to defend the life of the unborn and to render more human the lives of all our fellow human beings, wherever they may be.

And through the intercession of Our Lady of the Rosary, whose feast we celebrate today, may we come one day to the fullness of eternal life in Christ Jesus our Lord. Amen.

Christian Freedom

Homily of Pope John Paul II
During Mass Celebrated in the Sport Stadium
of Serravalle in San Marino
(August 29, 1982)

"Show us thy way, O Lord; and lead us on a level path" (*Ps.* 26:11). These words of the psalmist, which we sang before the Gospel, provide us with a starting point for our reflection on this Sunday's liturgy. At the same time, they provide me with an occasion to thank the Lord for having led me here, to the glorious Republic of San Marino, and for my being able to address to you, dear San Marinese, my most cordial greetings.

I would like to address a special greeting to the Captains Regent and to the other political and civil authorities present at this eucharistic celebration; I greet very warmly Bishop Giovanni Locatelli and, with him, all the priests and all the faithful of the Diocese of San Marino Montefeltro; I greet each of you and I thank you for the cordiality with which you have received me.

I am really delighted to be among you as the first Successor of Peter to visit this republic and I pray that this extraordinary ecclesiastical event will be a cause for gladness for all of you, and a salutary occasion to strengthen the foundations of your Christian being. My delight, however, has another source as well: my soul rejoices in perceiving and in breathing in that old and hearty, pure and noble atmosphere which belongs to institutions which have been tested by history, which have been able to face the centuries ever faithful to themselves, even while keeping pace with the changing world.

This land has never renounced its own freedom or its national and religious identity, drawing its inspiration from the figure of St. Marino, who is justly considered by tradition as being not only the protector but also the founder of your republic.

St. Marino is a highly evocative name for you San Marinese and for all. It calls up a long series of events and of noble—often epic—feats in defense of a civil autonomy always inspired by the values of the Christian faith. It is a name linked to the life of a holy Christian who was desirous of solitude, dedicated to prayer, vigorous in confronting the toils of work, and undefeated in his love for freedom.

It is not our task, especially in this solemn moment dedicated to eucharistic prayer, to investigate historical questions or even instructive episodes which are lost in a legendary halo fostered by a different sensitivity of times past. Here it is necessary to affirm, in accord with historical reality, that the cult dedicated to St. Marino since the first centuries of the Christian era and the free community which arose on Mount Titanus are linked to the eminent figure of an excellent follower of Christ who, having reached the light of truth and the life of grace, offered, even in public life, an evangelical witness as a layman coherent with his own faith and intrepid in its defense of human dignity.

Well-known to all of you are the words attributed to St. Marino, which he is said to have spoken before dying: "Filii, relinquo vos liberos" ("Children, I leave you free"). These words form, one might say, the fundamental historical, political and juridical ideal of your republic. These words, in their original context, referred to your community's territory and to its incipient institutions. In historical perspective, we see that these words gave rise to a political autonomy which is still intact today and which will continue vigorously into the future.

Rightly, thus, since the 11th century, when a more distinct sense of communal freedom was awakened and cities elected their own patrons, the people of the land, who had had for some time in St. Marino their own patron saint, began to invoke him as preserver and support, but most of all as *author of freedom.*

These same words, recorded above, the ideal fiber of San Marinese life, in the pastoral context of my visit today and even more in the liturgical context of this eucharistic celebration, evoke and announce your saint's own transcendent message of "Christian freedom," witnessed to under many circumstances by your ancestors and valid for every age until the end of time.

What is the Christian sense of this message of freedom?

This question is very important—indeed essential and unavoidable—because various and opposing interpretations exist of the meaning of "freedom," often with contrasting practical consequences.

For a genuine Christian concept of freedom, it is necessary to recall first of all the words of Jesus, directed to those who had believed in Him: "If you continue in my word, you are truly my disciples, and you will know the truth, and the truth will make you free. . . . Truly, truly I say to you, everyone who commits sin is a slave to sin. . . . So if the Son makes you free, you will be free indeed" (*Jn.* 8:31-36).

Jesus makes authentic freedom dependent more than anything on a consciousness of the whole truth of the mystery of God, announced and witnessed by Christ himself and then, as a consequence, on the putting away of evil, that is, of sin, transgression of the moral law.

St. Paul, who knew well both the word of the Lord and the drama of every man, because of the inmost dissension between good and evil, extolls the greatness and the richness of the freedom brought us by Christ (see *Gal.* 4:31), which consists of emancipation from the slavery of sin and from its law of death (see *Rom.* 6:22, 8:2 and 2 *Tim.* 4:18) and of the capacity to live according to the law of good, that is, according to the Spirit of God. The apostle, indeed, affirms categorically: "Where the Spirit of the Lord is, there is freedom" (2 *Cor.* 3:17).

If, then, freedom is God's greatest gift to man, created in His own image and thus rational and with free will, it is also the most precious fruit of the redemptive work of Christ, who made possible for man the interior autonomous option for good, even if this is not always realized by existential experience.

This gift of freedom involves heavy responsibility: the great duty which cannot be set aside, of adhering to the law of God, according to which the whole and perfect use of freedom is realized by him who is capable of drawing from it *the greatest love for others.* St. Paul is, once again, our authoritative teacher, with these words directed to the Galatians: "For you were called to freedom, brethren; only do not use your freedom as an opportunity for the flesh, but through love be servants of one another" (*Gal.* 3:13).

In the framework thus far delineated, allow me to repeat now what I wrote in my first encyclical: "The words of Jesus: 'You will know the truth and the truth will make you free,' contain both a fundamental requirement and a warning: the requirement of an honest relationship with regard to truth as a condition for authentic freedom, and the warning to avoid every kind of illusory freedom, every superficial unilateral freedom, every freedom that fails to enter into the whole truth about man and the world" (Encyclical Letter *Redemptor Hominis,* n. 12).

The use of freedom, in the light of the Christian truth and aided by grace, must thus become charity, love, donation; that is, it must bring forth the fruits of the Spirit: joy, peace, patience, benevolence, goodness . . . (see *Gal.* 5:22).

With an Augustinian phrase I say to you: The truth has set us free; charity must make us one another's servants!

Christian freedom, which is really "perpetual freedom" because it is founded on an acceptance of and respect for the eternal personal absolute God, is, however, continually menaced by errors and by behavior opposed to its roots and to its teleological dynamism delineated above.

What are the actual threats to Christian freedom? The errors of today and of always, that is atheistic, agnostic, or merely illuministic visions of life which lead, often because of unconfessed motives of power, to a dissolution of the transcendent values in the various institutions of the social framework, which are the foundations of freedom and of human dignity.

In a word, an areligious vision of history and of man leads to violation of the divine law and, thus, to the mistaken use of freedom.

St. James, in today's reading, recommends to us to "receive with meekness the implanted word" (*Jas.* 1:21) that is faith in God, who in Christ has come to us and has redeemed us. It is ever more necessary to make this faith bear fruit, and to accept its concrete demands. If the divine seeds of faith are left aside and only certain others are cultivated, these others show themselves sooner or later to be inadequate and insufficient.

On the other hand, in the fruit that matures from faith there is contained and ennobled whatever is derived also from other not illegitimate fruits.

This is valid in a particular and emblematic way for the life of the family, the fundamental cell of society, which is based on marriage. Marriage, indeed, was elevated by Christ to the dignity of sacrament in order to reinforce and sanctify the love of spouses which God, since the very origins of humanity, willed to be indissoluble and faithful like the institution that derives from it.

"What therefore God has joined together, let not man put asunder" *(Mk.* 10:9). The conjugal union cannot and must not be tampered with by any human authority. This is true whether marriage be considered in its natural or in its sacramental aspect.

For these reasons, the Church can neither change nor attenuate its teachings on marriage and the family; the Church deplores every attack, whether against the unity of marriage, or against its indissolubility, as in the case of divorce.

The Church also clearly affirms that marriage, by nature, must be open to the transmission of human life when Providence makes this gift, and must in every case be respectful of human life from conception onward. Such is the sublime procreative mission entrusted by God to the spouses. This mission involves, along with a very great responsibility, a sublime dignity guaranteed by God himself.

As regards the schools, it is necessary to offer to our youths, tomorrow's citizens, an education which takes into account those sublime truths which, honored by their forefathers, offer a secure and exhaustive response to the great questions of the human heart, liberating it from the spirals of anguish and of desperation and offering it, even, a sense of the utility of pain and of life's wearisome earthly journey.

Dear San Marinese, your community must remain faithful to the ideal patrimony built up over the centuries under the inspiration of its founder.

It is ever more necessary, in order to oppose the present threats to freedom, to form our consciences according to a Christian morality which is not merely superficial and exterior like that which Christ rejected in very strong terms in today's Gospel (see *Mt.* 7:21-23), but based on a respect for one's own freedom and that of others and, above all, on a respect for the holy will of God, who is the creator and provider of freedom. This requires austerity of life and faithfulnes in prayer, especially communal eucharistic prayer.

On such a ground let San Marino's future be constructed!

I wish the blessing of God on your way for today and the future and I commend you all to the Lord and to the greatness of His grace during this eucharistic celebration, "that you may be filled with all the fullness of God" (*Eph.* 3:19). Amen!

Religious Freedom: The Foundation of All Other Rights

On Saturday, March 10, 1984, the Holy Father received in audience two hundred participants in the Fifth International Colloquium of Juridical Studies sponsored by the Pontifical Lateran University on the twentieth anniversary of the encyclical Pacem in Terris. *The theme of the conference was "Basic Rights of the Human Person and Religious Freedom." The group was led by the rector of the Lateran University, Mons. Pietro Rossano, Auxiliary Bishop of Rome, and by Mons. Franco Biffi, who directed the work of the Colloquium.*

Following is a translation of John Paul II's address.

Dear Brothers,

1. I am very pleased by this meeting, because it offers me the opportunity to manifest to you my pleasure for your having chosen as the theme of your customary Juridical Colloquium such an important and relevant subject: "The fundamental rights of the human person and religious freedom," and for having combined the treatment of the subject with the commemoration of the election of John XXIII as Supreme Pontiff and the twentieth anniversary of his encyclical *Pacem in Terris.*

The competence and commitment of those who have spoken during the Colloquium are the guarantee of the sure seriousness of your work and of a positive contribution to a deeper study of the theme.

I wish to address my gratitude and cordial greeting to everyone: in a special way, to the distinguished speakers; to the Rector of the University, Mons. Pietro Rossano, who welcomed and encouraged the initiative, which has now become part of the normal life of the *Utriusque Iuris* Institute; and to Mons. Franco Biffi, who directed the work.

2. One of the signs of the times which greatly affects human coexistence and its ceaseless evolution is the more mature awareness which men throughout the world have acquired of their *dignity as persons.* It is a dignity which is existentially perceived as a fact of conscience and which, historically and culturally, is expressed through the progressive specification and claiming of human rights, proclaimed in solemn international declarations and now incorporated into the laws of modern nations.

It is precisely the dignity of the person, which today is ever more universally felt and proclaimed, that must be recognized as the meeting point for a fruitful, or rather, necessary, dialogue between the Church and the world of our era for building an authentic civilization based on truth and love. In fact, the voice of the Church, which echoes that of human conscience, must resound in the midst of various systems and most varied socio-cultural conditions, in order to educate persons and communities to form public opinion and guide the leaders of peoples.

3. Let us keep in mind, then, that the action of the Church in the field of human rights intends to remain always at the service of man; man as she conceives him in his anthropological view. In fact, she does not need to resort to systems and ideologies to love, to safeguard man's freedom and to collaborate for it. It is from the center of the Gospel, of which she is guardian and proclaimer, that she draws the inspiration and the criteria to work to make peace and justice grow against all slavery, violence and aggression against man and his rights. It is therefore not in order to befit the time nor to instrumentalize that the Church, "expert in humanity" (cf. Paul VI, *Discourse to the United Nations,* October 5, 1965), rises in defense of human rights. It is because of an authentic evangelical commitment, to which she remains faithful by keeping free in the face of opposing systems and by opting solely for man considered in his integral being.

The Lord Jesus in the parable of the Good Samaritan described the model for the care of human needs (cf. *Lk.* 10:20), and declared that he will identify himself with the least, to whom he will extend his hand (cf. *Mt.* 25:31 ff.). And the Church has learned and is learning from this and other pages of the Gospel (cf. *Mk.* 6:35-44) that an indispensable part of her evangelizing mission is the commitment to justice and to the work of man's advancement.

4. What criteria can we use in today's world to see if the rights of all persons are being safeguarded? What foundations can we offer as a basis upon which man's rights can flourish? Without doubt this basis is the dignity of the human person. My predecessor John XXIII explained it in this way in the encyclical *Pacem in Terris:* "In an orderly and fruitful coexistence the principle that every human being is a person must be placed as a foundation . . .; therefore, he is a subject of rights and duties which immediately and simultaneously flow from his very nature: rights and duties which are therefore universal, inviolable, inalienable."

It is in this dignity of the person that human rights find their immediate source. And it is respect for this dignity which gives rise to their effective protection. The human person, even when he errs, both man and woman, always maintains an inherent dignity which he never loses (cf.

Pacem in Terris, no. 158).

Therefore, believers must create the conditions for God to speak to man through the Church, to the end of contributing more authentically to the knowledge that all rights of the person stem from his dignity, firmly rooted in God.

5. Now among man's rights there is justly listed the right to religious freedom; rather, this is the most fundamental, since the dignity of every person has its first source in his essential relationship with God the Creator and Father, in whose image and likeness he was created, since he is endowed with intelligence and freedom.

The right to religious freedom has been present—as surely emerged also during your colloquium—in the life and history of the Church since its earliest times. The Second Vatican Council considered it particularly necessary to elaborate a broader declaration on this subject, the well-known *Dignitatis Humanae.* In this document there was expressed not only the theological concept of the problem, but also the concept from the point of view of natural right, that is, of the purely human position, on the basis of those premises dictated by man's very experience, by his reason and by the meaning of his dignity.

Certainly, the limitation of the religious freedom of individuals and communities not only is a painful experience for them, but above all strikes man's very dignity, regardless of the religion professed or of the concept which they have of the world. The above-mentioned Council document states what is such a limitation and violation of religious freedom, strongly emphasizing that man has the right to live in truth and in freedom to follow the ultimate meaning of his life.

This right is a human right and therefore universal; since it does not stem from the honest work of persons nor from their correct conscience, but from persons themselves, or rather, from their existential being which, in its constituent parts, is substantially identical in all persons. It is, therefore, a right which exists in every person and always exists, even in the hypothesis that it is not exercised or is violated by the very subject in whom it is inherent. In fact, the violation of a right does not mean its destruction, but brings to light its need to be reclaimed (cf. *Dignitatis Humanae,* no. 2).

6. It is, however, a right functioning as a duty. Rather, as my predecessor Paul VI repeated many times, it is the most fundamental of rights functioning as the first of duties, which is the duty to move toward God in the light of truth with that movement of the heart which is love, a movement which is illuminated and nourished only in that light (cf. Apostolic Exhortation *Evangelii Nuntiandi,* no. 39). "The disciple is bound by a grave obligation toward Christ his Master ever more adequately to

understand the truth received from him, faithfully to proclaim it, and vigorously to defend it, never—be it understood—having recourse to means that are incompatible with the spirit of the Gospel. At the same time, the charity of Christ urges him to act lovingly, prudently and patiently in his dealings with those who are in error or in ignorance with regard to the faith. All is to be taken into account—the Christian duty to Christ, the life-giving Word which must be proclaimed, the rights of the human person, and the measure of grace granted by God through Christ to men, who are invited freely to accept and profess the faith" (*Dignitatis Humanae,* no. 14). It is certainly an error to impose anything on man's conscience, but to propose to this conscience the Gospel truth and salvation in Christ Jesus with full clarity and with absolute respect for the free choices that the conscience will make, far from being an attack on religious freedom, is reverence for this freedom, to which is offered the choice of a way which even nonbelievers consider noble and exalting.

This respectful way of presenting Christ and his kingdom, besides being a right, is a duty of the evangelizer's.

In the face of so many humanisms, often included in a strictly economic, biological and psychical vision of man, the Church has the right and the duty to proclaim the truth about man, received from her Master himself, and to strive that Christ, God's gift to the world, may find the right of citizenship in the lives of individuals, of nations, of continents, in the life of all mankind.

Dear brothers, accept these considerations as a sign of my profound esteem for you and for your important work. May the Lord be generous to you with light and support, consoling your efforts with the joy of a deeper knowledge of the truth, which in him has its inexhaustible source. I accompany these wishes with my Blessing, for you and for your activity as scholars and teachers.

Charter of the Rights of the Family

Presented by the Holy See to all persons, institutions, and authorities concerned with the mission of the family in today's world—October 22, 1983.

INTRODUCTION

The well-being of families, strained today by the twin forces of individualism and state power, is acknowledged as the basis of any healthy society. In our day, because of the weakening of families, society is beset by a host of evils, from abortion and the suppression of parental rights in education, to chronic poverty and the neglect of the aged.

In response to this critical situation, the Pontifical Commission on the Family released, on October 22, 1983, a document of immediate and far-reaching significance for American society.

The Vatican Charter of Family Rights constitutes a blueprint for building a healthy, humane society founded on the integrity of family life. For Catholics and for non-Catholics, it should serve as a source of reflection and a guide to action in bringing the values of the Gospel to bear on secular life.

PREAMBLE—Considering that:

A. the rights of the person, even though they are expressed as rights of the individual, have a fundamental social dimension which finds an innate and vital expression in the family;

B. the family is based on marriage, that intimate union of life in complimentarity between a man and a woman which is constituted in the freely contracted and publicly expressed indissoluble bond of matrimony, and is open to the transmission of life;

C. marriage is the natural institution to which the mission of transmitting life is exclusively entrusted;

D. the family, a natural society, exists prior to the state or any other community, and possesses inherent rights which are inalienable;

E. the family constitutes, much more than a mere juridical, social, and economic unit, a community of love and solidarity, which is uniquely suited to teach and transmit cultural, ethical, social, spiritual, and religious values, essential for the development and well-being of its own members and of society;

F. the family is the place where different generations come together and help one another to grow in human wisdom and to harmonize the rights of individuals with other demands of social life;

G. the family and society, which are mutually linked by vital and organic bonds, have a complementary function in the defense and advancement of the good of every person and of humanity;

H. the experience of different cultures throughout history has shown the need for society to recognize and defend the institution of the family;

I. society, and in a particular manner the state and international organizations, must protect the family through measures of a political, economic, social and juridical character, which aim at consolidating the unity and stability of the family so that it can exercise its specific function;

J. the rights, the fundamental needs, the well-being and the values of the family, even though they are progressively safeguarded in some cases, are often ignored and not rarely undermined by laws, institutions, and socioeconomic programs;

K. many families are forced to live in situations of poverty which prevent them from carrying out their role with dignity;

L. the Catholic Church, aware that the good of the person, of society, and of the Church herself passes by way of the family, has always held it part of her mission to proclaim to all the plan of God instilled in human nature concerning marriage and the family, to promote these two institutions and to defend them against all those who attack them.

M. the Synod of Bishops celebrated in 1980 explicitly recommended that a "Charter of the Rights of the Family" be drawn up and circulated to all concerned; the Holy See, having consulted the Bishops' conferences, now presents this:

Charter of the Rights of the Family

And urges all states, international organizations, and all interested institutions and persons to promote respect for these rights, and to secure their effective recognition and observance.

ARTICLE 1 — All persons have the right to the free choice of their state of life and thus to marry and establish a family or to remain single.

a) Every man and every woman, having reached marriage age and having the necessary capacity, has the right to marry and establish a family without any discrimination whatsoever; legal restrictions to the exercise of this right, whether they be of a permanent or temporary nature, can be introduced only when they are required by grave and objective demands of the institution of marriage itself and its social and public significance; they must respect in all cases the dignity and the fundamental rights of the person.

b) Those who wish to marry and establish a family have the right to expect from society the moral, educational, social, and economic conditions which will enable them to exercise their right to marry in all maturity and responsibility.

c) The institutional value of marriage should be upheld by the public authorities; the situation of non-married couples must not be placed on the same level as marriage duly contracted.

ARTICLE 2 — Marriage cannot be contracted except by the free and full consent of the spouses duly expressed.

a) With due respect for the traditional role of the families in certain cultures in guiding the decision of their children, all pressure which would impede the choice of a specific person as spouse is to be avoided.

b) The future spouses have the right to their religious liberty. Therefore to impose as a prior condition for marriage a denial of faith or a profession of faith which is contrary to conscience, constitutes a violation of this right.

c) The spouses, in the natural complementarity which exists between man and woman, enjoy the same dignity and equal rights regarding the marriage.

ARTICLE 3 — The spouses have the inalienable right to found a family and to decide on the spacing of births and the number of children to be born, taking into full consideration their duties towards themselves, their children already born, the family and society, in a just hierarchy of values and in accordance with the objective moral order which excludes recourse to contraception, sterilization, and abortion.

a) The activities of public authorities and private organizations which attempt in any way to limit the freedom of couples in deciding about their children constitute a grave offense against human dignity and justice.

b) In international relations, economic aid for the advancement of peoples must not be conditioned on acceptance of programs of contraception, sterilization, and abortion.

c) The family has a right to assistance by society in the bearing and rearing of children. Those married couples who have a large family have a right to adequate aid and should not be subjected to discrimination.

ARTICLE 4 — Human life must be respected and protected absolutely from the moment of conception.

a) Abortion is a direct violation of the fundamental right to life of the human being.

b) Respect of the dignity of the human being excludes all experimental manipulation or exploitation of the human embryo.

c) All interventions on the genetic heritage of the human person that are not aimed at correcting anomalies constitute a violation of the right to bodily integrity and contradict the good of the family.

d) Children, both before and after birth, have the right to special protection and assistance, as do their mothers during pregnancy and for a reasonable period of time after childbirth.

e) All children, whether born in or out of wedlock, enjoy the same right to social protection, with a view to their integral personal development.

f) Orphans or children who are deprived of the assistance of their parents or guardians must receive particular protection on the part of society. The state, with regard to foster-care or adoption, must provide legislation which assists suitable families to welcome into their home children who are in need of permanent or temporary care. This legislation must, at the same time, respect the natural rights of the parents.

g) Children who are handicapped have the right to find in the home and the school an environment suitable to their human development.

ARTICLE 5 — Since they have conferred life on their children, parents have the original, primary, and inalienable right to educate them; hence they must be acknowledged as the first and foremost educators of their children.

a) Parents have the right to educate their children in conformity with their moral and religious convictions, taking into account the cultural traditions of the family which favor the good and the dignity of the child; they should also receive from society the necessary aid and assistance to perform their educational role properly.

b) Parents have the right to choose freely schools or other means necessary to educate their children in keeping with their convictions. Public authorities must ensure that public subsidies are so allocated that parents are truly free to exercise this right without incurring unjust burdens. Parents should not have to sustain, directly or indirectly, extra charges which would deny or unjustly limit the exercise of this freedom.

c) Parents have the right to ensure that their children are not compelled to attend classes which are not in agreement with their own moral and religious convictions. In particular, sex education is a basic right of the parents and must always be carried out under their close supervision, whether at home or in educational centers chosen and controlled by them.

d) The rights of parents are violated when a compulsory system of education is imposed by the state from which all religious formation is excluded.

e) The primary right of parents to educate their children must be upheld in all forms of collaboration between parents, teachers, and school authorities, and particularly in forms of participation designed to give citizens a voice in the functioning of schools and in the formulation and implementation of educational policies.

f) The family has the right to expect that the means of social communication will be positive instruments for the building up of society, and will reinforce the fundamental values of the family. At the same time the family has the right to be adequately protected, especially with regard to its youngest members, from the negative effects and misuse of the mass media.

ARTICLE 6 — The family has the right to exist and to progress as a family.

a) Public authorities must respect and foster the dignity, lawful independence, privacy, integrity, and stability of every family.

b) Divorce attacks the very institution of marriage and of the family.

c) The extended family system, where it exists, should be held in esteem and helped to carry out better its traditional role of solidarity and mutual assistance, while at the same time respecting the rights of the nuclear family and the personal dignity of each member.

ARTICLE 7 — Every family has the right to live freely its own domestic religious life under the guidance of the parents, as well as the right to profess publicly and to propagate the faith, to take part in public worship and in freely chosen programs of religious instruction, without suffering discrimination.

ARTICLE 8 — The family has the right to exercise its social and political function in the construction of society.

a) Families have the right to form associations with other families and institutions, in order to fulfill the family's role suitably and effectively, as well as to protect the rights, foster the good, and represent the interests of the family.

b) On the economic, social, juridical, and cultural levels, the rightful role of families and family associations must be recognized in the planning and development of programs which touch on family life.

ARTICLE 9 — Families have the right to be able to rely on an adequate family policy on the part of public authorities in the juridical, economic, social, and fiscal domains, without any discrimination whatsoever.

a) Families have the right to economic conditions which assure them a standard of living appropriate to their dignity and full development. They should not be impeded from acquiring and maintaining private possessions which would favor suitable family life; the laws concerning inheritance or transmission of property must respect the needs and rights of family members.

b) Families have the right to measures in the social domain which take into account their needs, especially in the event of the premature death of one or both parents, of the abandonment of one of the spouses, or accident, or sickness or invalidity, in the case of unemployment, or whenever the family has to bear extra burdens on behalf of its members for reasons of old age, physical or mental handicaps, or the education of children.

c) The elderly have the right to find within their own family or, when this is not possible, in suitable institutions, an environment which will enable them to live their later years of life in serenity while pursuing those activities which are compatible with their age and which enable them to participate in social life.

d) The rights and necessities of the family, and especially the value of family unity, must be taken into consideration in penal legislation and policy, in such a way that a detainee remains in contact with his or her family and the family is adequately sustained during the period of detention.

ARTICLE 10 — Families have a right to a social and economic order in which the organization of work permits the members to live together, and does not hinder the unity, well-being, health and the stability of the family, while offering also the possibility of wholesome recreation.

a) Remuneration for work must be sufficient for establishing and maintaining a family with dignity, either through a suitable salary, called a "family wage," or through other social measures such as family allowances or the remuneration of the work in the home of one of the parents; it should be such that mothers will not be obliged to work outside the home to the detriment of family life and especially of the education of the children.

b) The work of the mother in the home must be recognized and respected because of its value for the family and for society.

ARTICLE 11 — The family has the right to decent housing, fitting for family life and commensurate to the number of the members, in a physical environment that provides the basic services for the life of the family and the community.

ARTICLE 12 — The families of migrants have the right to the same protection as that accorded other families.

a) The families of immigrants have the right to respect for their own culture and to receive suppport and assistance towards their integration into the community to which they contribute.

b) Emigrant workers have the right to see their family united as soon as possible.

c) Refugees have the right to the assistance of public authorities and international organizations in facilitating the reunion of their families.

Marriage and the Family

Address delivered by Pope John Paul II
to 14 U.S. bishops making their ad limina visit
(September 24, 1983)

It is a real joy for me to welcome you to this collegial gathering in which we come together in the name of Christ, who is "the chief Shepherd" (1 *Pt.* 5:4) of the Church and the Lord and Savior of us all. As we assemble here on the occasion of your *ad limina* visit, I wish to reflect with you on one of the most important areas of our common pastoral responsibility: *Christian marriage and family life.*

In the pastoral constitution *Gaudium et Spes,* the bishops of the Second Vatican Council stated that "the well-being of the individual person and of human and Christian society is intimately linked with the healthy condition of the communion set up by marriage and the family" (*Gaudium et Spes* n. 47). We are all aware of *certain contemporary trends* which seem to threaten the stability, if not the very existence, of the family: a shift of emphasis toward the comfort of the individual over the well-being of the family as society's basic social unit, increasing divorce rates, attitudes of sexual permissiveness and the suggestion that other types of relationships can replace marriage and the family.

In the face of these attitudes we have the *important mission of proclaiming Christ's Good News about Christian married love,* the identity and worth of the family, and the importance of its mission in the Church and in the world. Accordingly, in *Familiaris Consortio,* I noted that the bishop should exercise particular solicitude for the family, "devoting to it personal interest, care, time, personnel and resources, but, above all, personal support for the families and for all those who, in the various diocesan structures, assist him in the pastoral care of the family" (*ibid.,* n. 73).

This pastoral responsibility is based on the fact that *Christian family life is founded on the Sacrament of Marriage,* which is "the specific source and original means of sanctification for Christian couples and families" (*ibid.,* n. 56). It is up to us, together with our priests, to offer to the faithful the richness of the Church's teaching on the Sacrament of Marriage. This teaching, when explained well, is so very powerful, presenting as it does the covenant of God's relationship with His people and of *Christ's relationship with the Church.* It is of extreme importance for

Christian couples to be aware of the divine truth that, in their human love elevated and sanctified by sacramental marriage, they actually "signify and partake in the fruitful love between Christ and His Church" (*Lumen Gentium,* 11).

Because Christian marriage expresses the relationship of Christ and the Church, it possesses the qualities of *unity,* permanence or indissolubility, fidelity and fruitfulness. In the words of the Second Vatican Council we proclaim: "The intimate partnership of married life and love has been established by the Creator and qualified by His laws, and is rooted in the conjugal covenant of irrevocable personal consent. Hence, by that human act whereby spouses mutually bestow and accept each other a relationship arises which, by divine will and in the eyes of society, too, is a lasting one" (*Gaudium et Spes* n. 48).

The primary responsibilities of married couples are described in both *Gaudium et Spes* and *Humanae Vitae* in terms of *developing conjugal love* and *pursuing responsible parenthood.* Basic to the marriage relationship is that special interpersonal love which the spouses give to one another. The Church proclaims this conjugal love as eminently human, involving the good of the whole person and enriching and ennobling both husband and wife in their Christian life. This love creates a special unity between a man and woman, resembling the unity between Christ and His Church. *Gaudium et Spes* assures us that married love is caught up in God's love and is affected by Christ's redemptive power and the saving activity of the Church. As a result, the spouses are led to God and assisted and strengthened in the sublime role of being a father or mother (cf. *ibid.* no. 48).

Marriage is also directed toward building a family. The spouses share with God in the continuing work of creation. Conjugal love is rooted in divine love, and is meant to be creative and life sustaining. It is through spiritual union and the union of their bodies that the couple fulfills its procreative role by giving life, love and a sense of security to children.

Giving life and helping children to reach maturity through *education* are among the *primary privileges and responsibilities* of married couples. We know that married couples usually look forward to parenthood, but are sometimes impeded from achieving their hopes and desires by social conditions, by personal circumstances or even by the inability to beget new life. But the Church encourages couples to be generous and hopeful, to realize that parenthood is a privilege and that each child bears witness to the couple's own love for each other, to their generosity and to their openness to God. They must be encouraged to see the child as an enrichment of their marriage and a gift of God to themselves and to their other children.

Couples should thoughtfully and prayerfully make their decisions regarding the spacing of births and the size of their families. In pursuing these decisions they need to be attentive to the teaching of the Church regarding the *inherent connection between the unitive and procreative dimensions of the marriage act* (cf. *Humanae Vitae,* 12). Couples must be urged to avoid any action that threatens a life already conceived, that denies or frustrates their procreative power, or violates the integrity of the marriage act.

As bishops, together with your priests and others in the family apostolate, you are called upon to help couples know and understand the reasons for *the Church's teaching on human sexuality.* This teaching can be understood only in the light of God's plan for human love and marriage as they relate to creation and redemption. Let us often present to our people the uplifting and exhilarating affirmation of human love, telling them that "God inscribed in the humanity of man and woman the vocation, and thus the capacity and responsibility, of love and communion. Love is, therefore, the fundamental and innate vocation of every human being" (*Familiaris Consortio,* 11).

Thus, in order to avoid any trivialization or desecration of sexuality, we must teach that sexuality transcends the purely biological sphere and concerns the innermost being of the human person as such. Sexual love is truly human only if it is an integral part of the love by which a man and a woman commit themselves totally to one another until death. *This full self-giving is possible only in marriage.*

It is this teaching, based on the Church's understanding of the dignity of the human person and the fact that *sex is a gift of God,* that must be communicated to both married and engaged couples, and, indeed, to the whole Church. This teaching must be at the basis of all education in sexuality and chastity. It must be communicated to parents, who have the primary responsibility for the education of their children, and also to pastors and religious teachers, who collaborate with parents in the fulfillment of their responsibility.

A special and important part of your ministry to families has to do with *natural family planning.* The number of couples successfully using the natural methods is constantly growing. A much more concerted effort is needed, however. As stated in *Familiaris Consortio:* "The ecclesial community at the present time must take on the task of instilling conviction and offering practical help to those who wish to live out their parenthood in a truly responsible way. . . . This implies a broader, more decisive and more systematic effort to make the natural methods of regulating fertility known, respected and applied" (*ibid.,* n. 35).

Those couples who choose the natural methods perceive the profound difference—both anthropological and moral—between contraception and natural family planning. Yet, they may experience difficulties; indeed, they often go through a certain conversion in becoming committed to the use of the natural methods, and they stand in need of competent instruction, encouragement and pastoral counseling and support. We must be sensitive to their struggles and have a feeling for the needs they experience. We must encourage them to continue their efforts with generosity, confidence and hope. As bishops we have the charism and the pastoral responsibility to make our people aware of the unique influence *that the grace of the Sacrament of Marriage has on every aspect of married life, including sexuality* (cf. *Familiaris Consortio,* 33). The teaching of Christ's Church is not only light and strength for God's people, but it uplifts their hearts in gladness and hope.

Your episcopal conference has established a special program to expand and coordinate efforts in the various dioceses. But the success of such an effort requires the abiding pastoral interest and support of each bishop in his own diocese, and I am deeply grateful to you for what you do in this important apostolate.

The family is rightly described as the *domestic Church.* As such, it transmits the faith and the Christian value system from one generation to the next. Parents are called to be involved in the education of their children, precisely as young Christians. The family is also the center of sacramental catechesis. Increasingly, parents are called upon to take an active role in preparing their children for Baptism, First Confession and First Communion. Married couples are also active in programs of marriage preparation. All of this touches *the role of the family in sharing in the life and mission of the Church.* With all our hearts we should encourage family prayer and a family sacramental life, centered around the Eucharist. For the vitality of the Christian family derives from its union with Christ in the life of grace, which is nourished by the liturgy and by family prayer.

The Christian family also has a responsibility to participate in *the development of society.* As bishops in the United States you have *a long history of devoted* service to families *with special needs,* particularly through your Catholic social service agencies. Your diocesan agencies have also shown a special concern for the poor, for racial, ethnic and cultural minorities, as well as for the disadvantaged. But as the 1980 Synod of Bishops urged, and as was pointed out in *Familiaris Consortio,* "the social role of families is called upon to find expression also in the form of *political intervention;* families should be the first to take steps to see that the laws and institutions of the state not only do not offend but support and positively defend the rights and duties of the family" (*ibid.*, no 44). Your episcopal conference has been diligent in fostering this role through its pro-life activity, and especially the annual *Respect Life Program,* which begins next week for the current year.

The pastoral challenge is great, and it requires your personal and constant leadership, the collaboration of priests and Religious, and the generous and dedicated efforts of the Catholic laity, especially families. In a country as vast as yours, the task is very complex. But again I commend to you the recommendations of *Familiaris Consortio,* that is, that the episcopal conferences should formulate a *Directory for the Pastoral Care for the Family,* which will include the content of the preparation for marriage, and that priests and seminarians will be given special preparation for pastoral work with families. Specifically, for this reason, a special institute has been established for the study of marriage and family life at the Pontifical Lateran University.

I am aware of your many other pastoral responsibilities and concerns, but from my pastoral journeys I am very much convinced of the vitality of Christian family life even in the face of so many tensions and pressures. I urge you to show the family special love and concern, to collaborate with others in supporting family life, and to proclaim constantly to your people that "the future of humanity passes by way of the family" (*Familiaris Consortio,* 86).

We simply cannot accept the contemporary pursuit of exaggerated convenience and comfort, for as Christians we must heed the vigorous exhortation of St. Paul: "Do not conform yourselves to this age" (*Rom.* 12:2). We must realize that in our struggles to overcome the negative influences of modern society we are identified with Christ the Lord, who by His suffering and death has redeemed the world. Thus, we can better impart to our people the message of the Second Vatican Council that in following Christ, who is the principle of life, "by the sacrifices and joys of their vocation and through their faithful love, married people will become witnesses of the mystery of love which the Lord revealed to the world by His death and resurrection" (*Gaudium et Spes,* 52).

Yes, dear brothers, *marriage and the family are closely linked to the Paschal Mystery* of the Lord Jesus. And human conjugal love remains for ever a great sacramental expression of the fact that "Christ loved the Church and gave himself up for her" (*Eph.* 5:25). In the power of the Holy Spirit let us communicate this gift of God's truth to the world.

The proclamation of this truth is our contribution to married couples; it is the proof of our pastoral love for families; and it will be the source of immense vitality for the Church of God in this generation and for gen-

erations yet to come. With determination, confidence and hope let us proclaim Christ's Good News for married love and family life. And may Mary, the Mother of Jesus, be with us in this apostolic task.

Lourdes Homily on Religious Freedom

At the feet of Our Lady of Lourdes, the Holy Father, immediately after the candlelight procession on the evening of 14 August 1983, delivered the following address, stressing one of his strong preoccupations: religious freedom in the world as an indispensable right of man, the fountain of hope.

1. On this peaceful evening, we keep vigil. We keep vigil while waiting to celebrate the glory of Mary. And we pray, no longer alone and in secret, but as a large nation following in the steps of the Risen Christ, lighting each other's way, encouraging each other, relying on faith in Christ Jesus and in his words which enlighten our hearts. Jesus tells us: "Let your lamps be burning ready" (*Lk.* 12:35): the lamp of faith and the lamp of prayer! Like the flames of our candles, may our prayer rise to God as one, to offer him, with Mary, our fervent thanksgiving, and to present together one vast entreaty.

Everyone has brought here some personal intentions, for his own salvation, for his family, for his community, for his country. That is good. This evening, we are putting all these requests together to entrust them, through Mary, to our heavenly Father. And we include also the intentions of the entire Church and of the entire world, seeking what corresponds to the will of God and not to ours alone.

Yes, for the entire world! May they find a place in our prayer those men and women, wherever they may be, who suffer from famine or other disasters, from the ravages of war, from the movement of populations; those who are the victims of terrorism, whether political or not, which strikes indiscriminately at the innocent, the victims of hatred, various forms of oppression, injustices of all kinds, those who are kidnapped, imprisoned illegally, tortured, condemned without recourse to justice; all those who suffer intolerable attacks on their human dignity and fundamental rights, who are prevented from expressing themselves freely in thought and in action, who are humiliated in their legitimate national aspirations; so that the attitude of those responsible may change and the victims may receive strength and courage. Let us think also of the moral distress of those who are lured into corruption of all kinds. And let us pray for those who are undergoing serious difficulties because of immigration, unemployment, sickness, infirmity or loneliness. Christ, *the Son of Man,* suffers in them. If I do not say more about these human miseries, it is because I often speak about them.

Likewise, as Christians, we are especially concerned in our prayer with the spiritual needs of the universal Church, whose needs you know well and which I often recall: conversion, the handing on of the faith, holiness of consecrated souls, vocations, the example of Christian families . . . But there is one especially glaring spiritual problem on which we will now focus our attention and prayer: *those who suffer for their faith.* All of us here who can freely express our faith and our prayer, let us make sure we do not forget these brothers and sisters of ours! And especially in this sanctuary of Lourdes towards which the eyes of the entire Christian world are turned since the Virgin Mary gave us new hope here. As Pope, carrying the concerns of all the Churches and often informed of their situation, I ask you to meditate with me on this mystery of the persecution of believers, by taking up again with Mary the words of Jesus.

2. "Blest are you when they insult you and persecute you and utter every kind of slander against you because of me. Be glad and rejoice, for your reward is great in heaven" (*Mt.* 5:11-12).

This beatitude, the last of the eight found in the Gospel of Matthew, I want to pronounce it before you, O Mother of Christ and of the Church, here at Lourdes. And, in saying it, I want to bring into your presence *all those,* wherever they may be, *who suffer persecution* "because of Christ," all those who are hated "because of my name" (cf. *Mk.* 13:13).

3. Christ spoke quite often to his disciples about persecutions. He made it clear to them that *persecution* would often be the price they would pay in giving witness before men (cf. *Lk.* 21:13).

At this time, let us recall some words of the Lord which reveal the true gospel of persecution:

"They will hand you over to the courts. You will be beaten in synagogues. You will be arraigned before governors and kings on my account and have to testify to your faith before them . . . Nonetheless, the man who holds out till the end is the one who will come through safe" (*Mk.* 13:9-13). However, "do not fear those who deprive the body of life *but cannot destroy the soul"* (*Mt.* 10:28).

Such are the words taken from the *Gospel of Mark and Matthew.*

The Gospel of Luke, in turn, after speaking of those who are hated, rejected and insulted *because of the Son of Man* (cf. *Lk.* 6:22-23), states clearly: "When they bring you before synagogues, rulers and authorities, do not worry about how to defend yourselves or what to say. The Holy Spirit will teach you at that moment all that should be said" (*Lk.* 12:11-12).

4. *We read also in the Gospel of John:*
"If you find that the world hates you, know it has hated me before you.
. . . The reason it hates you is that you do not belong to the world. But I chose you out of the world.
. . . No slave is greater than his master. They will harry you as they harried me . . . All this they will do to you because of my name, for they know nothing of him who sent me" (*Jn.* 15:18-21).
"I tell you all this that in me you may find peace. *You will suffer in the world.* But take courage! *I have overcome the world" (Jn.* 16:33).
5. Christ, then, prepared his disciples for persecution. In fact, they were harassed as soon as they started to carry out the mission given to them. *In Jerusalem,* the Apostles and those who believed in Christ were already being persecuted. The first three centuries of Christianity in the Roman Empire were the period of persecutions, the first of which broke out *in Rome* under Nero around the year 65. The Apostles Peter and Paul were among its many victims. Until the beginning of the fourth century, bloody persecutions repeated themselves regularly. *The Church was born on the Cross and grew up in the midst of persecutions.*
This is the way it was at the beginning, *in ancient Roman times.*
This is also the way it was later. Throughout the centuries, persecutions have broken out against the Church in various places, and the followers of Christ have given their lives for the faith and suffered the worst tortures.
The *martyrology* of the Church was put together over many centuries.
6. Today, during my pilgrimage to Lourdes, I would like to reach out in thought and with the heart of the Church to all those who suffer *persecution in our days.* I would like to reach out to all of them, through the heart of the Church, with the maternal Heart of the mother of God, venerated by the Church as his Mother and as the Queen of martyrs.
Persecutions today are often similar to those described in the Martyrology of the Church for past centuries. They include various types of discrimination against believers and against the whole community of the Church. Such forms of *discrimination* are often practiced at the same time as is recognized the right to religious liberty and to freedom of conscience, and this in the laws of individual countries as well as in declarations of an international nature. .
7. Must I be more specific?
In the persecutions of the early centuries, the usual penalties were death, deportation and exile.
Today, besides prison, concentration camps, forced labour camps and expulsion from one's country, there are other punishments less well

known but more subtle: not *violent* death, but a kind of *civil* death; not only isolation in prisons or in camps, but social discrimination or permanent restriction of personal liberty.

There are today hundreds upon hundreds of thousands of witnesses to the faith, all too often ignored or forgotten by public opinion whose attention is drawn elsewhere. They are often known to God alone. They suffer daily hardships, in various parts of every continent.

They include believers forced to meet in hiding because their religious community is not legally authorized.

They include bishops, priests and religious who are forbidden to exercise their sacred ministry in churches or in public gatherings.

They include nuns who have been dispersed and cannot live their consecrated life.

They include generous young men who are prevented from entering a seminary or religious house of formation to pursue their vocation.

They include young women who are denied the possibility of consecrating themselves to a common life dedicated to prayer or to works of charity.

They include parents who are refused the right to have their children educated according to their faith.

They include men and women, manual workers, intellectuals, or those carrying out other occupations, who, simply because they profess their faith, run the risk of being deprived of interesting opportunities for their careers or their studies.

To these cases can be added the serious and distressing condition of prisoners, internees and exiles, not only among Catholics and other Christians, but also among other believers (cf. *Redemptor Hominis,* 17). Their plight is like a hymn which rises continually to God from the sanctuary of their conscience, like a spiritual offering certainly pleasing to God.

8. All this must not make us forget that there are other difficulties in living the faith. They are not due only to external restrictions on freedom or to constraints by men, laws or regimes. They can also come from customs and ways of thinking which are contrary to evangelical principles and which have a powerful influence on society. Again, it could be the influence of materialism and of religious indifference which kill spiritual aspirations; or the false and individualistic notion of freedom which confuses the possibility of choosing whatever gratifies one's passions with the concern for fully developing one's human calling, spiritual destiny, and the common good. It is not this kind of freedom which forms the basis of human dignity and encourages Christian faith (cf. *Redemptor Hominis,* 12). Believers who are surrounded by such influences need

great courage to remain sane and faithful, and to exercise their freedom properly. We must pray for them also. As Jesus said, fear those who can destroy the soul (cf. *Mt.* 10:28).

9. In every age, the Church has had special *care,* special remembrance, and special *love* for those who "suffer for the name of Christ." This is evidence of lasting remembrance and constant concern on the part of the Church.

Our meeting today in Lourdes, at the feet of the Immaculate Mother of Christ, allows us to express this remembrance in a *special way.* Let us pray for all those who are persecuted in some way or other because of their faith, wherever they may be.

We have recalled the words of Christ himself. May these brothers and sisters find inspiration and strength in these words! *May the Holy Spirit be with them,* this Spirit who enlightens the mind and gives heroic courage to those who confess the faith. In a way, in the eyes of God, they shine as so many lights scattered throughout the world, giving strength to the Church in a mysterious way. May they all maintain interior peace and truly Christian strength of mind! May the sense of dignity which comes from interior *fidelity to conscience and truth* grow ever stronger in them! And may the Lord give them the grace of forgiving their persecutors and of loving their enemies!

O Mother of Christ, you who stood at the foot of the Cross of your Son, be close to all those who suffer persecution in the world today! May *your motherly presence* help them to bear their sufferings and to gain victory by the Cross!

The Role of Evangelization

The work of the Third Conference of Latin American Bishops began, in January of 1979, at a solemn gathering in the Major Palafoxian Seminary at Puebla de Los Angeles, Mexico. Pope John Paul II pronounced the opening address in the presence of all the bishops of Latin America:

Beloved Brothers in the Episcopate,

This hour that I have the happiness to experience with you is certainly an historic one for the Church in Latin America. World opinion is aware of this, as are the faithful members of your local Churches, and especially you yourselves are aware of it, you who will be the protagonists and leaders of this hour.

It is also an hour of grace, marked by the drawing near of the Lord, by a very special presence and action of the Spirit of God. For this reason we have confidently invoked that Spirit, at the beginning of our work. For this reason also I now wish to implore you, as a brother to very beloved brothers: all the days of this conference and in every one of its acts, let yourselves be led by the Spirit, open yourselves to his inspiration and his impulse, let it be he and no other spirit that guides and strengthens you.

Under the guidance of this Spirit, for the third time in the last 25 years you, the bishops of all the countries representing the Episcopate of the Continent of Latin America, have gathered together to study more deeply together the meaning of your mission in the face of the new demands of your peoples.

The Conference that is now opening, convoked by the revered Paul VI, confirmed by my unforgettable predecessor John Paul I, and reconfirmed by myself as one of the first acts of my pontificate, is linked with the Conference now long past, held in Rio de Janeiro, which had as its most notable result the birth of CELAM. But it is linked even more closely with the second Conference, of Medellin, of which it marks the tenth anniversary.

In these last ten years, how much progress humanity has made, and, with humanity and at its service, how much progress the Church has made! This third Conference cannot disregard that reality. It will therefore have to take as its point of departure the conclusions of Medellin, with all the positive elements that they contained, but without ignoring the incorrect interpretations at times made and which call for calm discernment, opportune criticism, and clear choices of position. You will be guided in your debates by the Working Document, prepared with such care so as to constitute the constant point of reference.

But you will also have at hand Paul VI's Apostolic Exhortation *Evangelii Nuntiandi.* With what care the great Pontiff approved as the Conference's theme: "The present and the future of evangelization in Latin America"!

Those who were close to him during the months when the Assembly was being prepared can tell you this. They can also bear witness to the gratitude with which he learned that the basic material of the whole Conference would be this text, into which he put his whole pastoral soul, as his life drew to a close. Now that he has "closed his eyes to this world's scene" (Testament of Paul VI), this document becomes a spiritual testament that the Conference will have to scrutinize with love and diligence, in order to make it the other obligatory point of reference, and in order to see how to put it into practice. The whole Church is grateful to you for giving, for what you are doing, and what other local Churches will perhaps do in their turn.

The Pope wishes to be with you at the beginning of your labours, and he is thankful to the Father of lights from whom comes down every perfect gift (cf. *James* 1:17), for having been able to be with you at yesterday's Solemn Mass, under the maternal gaze of the Virgin of Guadalupe, as also at the Mass this morning. I would very much like to stay with you in prayer, reflection and work: be sure that I shall stay with you in spirit, while the "anxiety for all the churches" (2 *Cor.* 11:28) calls me elsewhere. I wish at least, before continuing my pastoral visit through Mexico and before my return to Rome, to leave you as a pledge of my spiritual presence a few words, uttered with the solicitous care of a Pastor and the affection of a Father; words which are the echo of my main preoccupations regarding the theme you have to deal with and regarding the life of the Church in these beloved countries.

It is a great consolation for the universal Father to note that you come together here not as a symposium of experts, not as a parliament of politicians, not as a congress of scientists or technologists, however important such assemblies may be, but as a fraternal encounter of Pastors of the Church. And as Pastors you have the vivid awareness that your principal duty is to be Teachers of the Truth. Not a human and rational truth, but the Truth that comes from God, the Truth that brings with it the principle of the authentic liberation of man: "you will know the truth, and the truth will make you free" (*Jn.* 8:32); that Truth which is the only one that offers a solid basis for an adequate "praxis."

I.1 To be watchful for purity of doctrine, the basis in building up the Christian community, is therefore, together with the proclamation of the Gospel, the primary and irreplaceable duty of the pastor, of the Teacher of the faith. How often Saint Paul emphasized this, convinced as he was of the seriousness of the accomplishment of this duty (cf. 1 *Tim.* 1:3-7; 18-20; 4:11, 16; 2 *Tim.* 1:4-14). Over and above unity in love, unity in truth is always urgent for us. The beloved Pope Paul VI, in the Apostolic Exhortation *Evangelii Nuntiandi,* said: "The Gospel entrusted to us is also the word of truth. A truth which liberates and which alone gives peace of heart is what people are looking for when we proclaim the Good News to them. The truth about God, about man and his mysterious destiny, about the world . . . The preacher of the Gospel will therefore be a person who even at the price of personal renunciation and suffering always seeks the truth that he must transmit to others. He never betrays or hides truth out of a desire to please men, in order to astonish or to shock, nor for the sake of originality or a desire to make an impression . . . We are the pastors of the faithful people, and our pastoral service impels us to preserve, defend, and to communicate the truth regardless of the sacrifices that this involves" (*Evangelii Nuntiandi,* 78).

I.2 From you, Pastors, the faithful of your countries expect and demand above all a careful and zealous transmission of the truth concerning Jesus Christ. This truth is at the centre of evangelization and constitutes its essential content: "There is no true evangelization if the name, the teaching, the life, the promises, the Kingdom and the mystery of Jesus of Nazareth, the Son of God are not proclaimed" (*Evangelii Nuntiandi,* 22).

From the living knowledge of this truth will depend the vigour of the faith of millions of people. From it will also depend the strength of their support of the Church and of their active presence as Christians in the world. From this knowledge there will derive choices, values, attitudes and modes of behaviour capable of orienting and defining our Christian life and of creating new people, and hence a new humanity, for the conversion of the individual and social conscience (cf. *Evangelii Nuntiandi,* 18).

It is from a solid Christology that there must come light on so many doctrinal and pastoral themes and questions that you intend to study in these coming days.

I.3 And then we have to confess Christ before history and the world with a conviction that is profound, deeply felt and lived, just as Peter confessed him: "You are the Christ the Son of the living God" (*Mt.* 16:16.)

This is the Good News in a certain sense unique: the Church lives by it and for it, just as she draws from it everything that she has to offer to people, without any distinction of nation, culture, race, time, age or condition. For this reason "from that confession of faith (Peter's) the sacred history of salvation and of the People of God could not fail to take on a new dimension" (Homily of Pope John Paul II at the solemn inauguration of his Pontificate, 22 October 1978).

This is the one Gospel, and "even if we, or an angel from heaven, should preach to you a gospel contrary to that which we preached to you, let him be accursed," as the Apostle wrote in very clear terms (*Gal.* 1:8).

I.4 In fact, today there occur in many places—the phenomenon is not a new one—"re-readings" of the Gospel, the result of theoretical speculations rather than authentic meditation on the word of God and a true commitment to the Gospel. They cause confusion by diverging from the central criteria of the faith of the Church, and some people have the temerity to pass them on, under the guise of catechesis, to the Christian communities.

In some cases either Christ's divinity is passed over in silence, or some people in fact fall into forms of interpretation at variance with the Church's faith. Christ is said to be merely a "prophet," one who proclaimed God's Kingdom and love, but not the true Son of God, and therefore not the centre and object of the very Gospel message.

In other cases people claim to show Jesus as politically committed, as one who fought against Roman oppression and the authorities, and also as one involved in the class struggle. The idea of Christ as a political figure, a revolutionary, as the subversive man from Nazareth, does not tally with the Church's catechesis. By confusing the insidious pretexts of Jesus' accusers with the—very different—attitude of Jesus himself, some people adduce as the cause of his death the outcome of a political conflict, and nothing is said of the Lord's will to deliver himself and of his consciousness of his redemptive mission. The Gospels clearly show that for Jesus anything that would alter his mission as the Servant of Yahweh was a temptation (cf. *Mt.* 4:8; *Lk.* 4:5). He does not accept the position of those who mixed the things of God with merely political attitudes (cf. *Mt.* 22:21; *Mk.* 12:17; *Jn.* 18:36). He unequivocally rejects recourse to violence. He opens his message of conversion to everybody, without excluding the very Publicans. The perspective of his mission is much deeper. It consists in complete salvation through a transforming, peacemaking, pardoning and reconciling love. There is no doubt, moreover, that all this is very demanding for the attitude of the Christian who wishes truly to serve his least brethren, the poor, the needy, the emarginated; in a word, all those who in their lives reflect the sorrowing face of the Lord (cf. *Lumen Gentium,* 8).

I.5 Against such *re-readings* therefore, and against the perhaps brilliant but fragile and inconsistent hypotheses flowing from them, *Evangelization in the present and future of Latin America* cannot cease to affirm the Church's faith: Jesus Christ, the Word and the Son of God, becomes man in order to come close to man and to offer him, through the power of his mystery, salvation, the great gift of God (cf. *Evangelii Nuntiandi,* 19 and 27).

This is the faith that has permeated your history and has formed the best of the values of your peoples and must go on animating, with every energy, the dynamism of their future. This is the faith that reveals the vocation to harmony and unity that must drive away the dangers of war in this continent of hope, in which the Church has been such a powerful factor of integration. This is the faith, finally, which the faithful people of Latin America through their religious practices and popular piety express with such vitality and in such varied ways.

From this faith in Christ, from the bosom of the Church, we are able to serve men and women, our peoples, and to penetrate their culture with the Gospel, to transform hearts, and to make systems and structures more human.

Any form of silence, disregard, mutilation or inadequate emphasis of the whole of the Mystery of Jesus Christ that diverges from the Church's faith cannot be the valid content of evangelization. "Today, under the pretext of a piety that is false, under the deceptive appearance of a preaching of the Gospel, some people are trying to deny the Lord Jesus," wrote a great Bishop in the midst of the hard crises of the fourth century. And he added: "I speak the truth, so that the cause of the confusion that we are suffering may be known to all. I cannot keep silent" (Saint Hilary of Poitiers, *Contra Auxentium,* 1-4). Nor can you, the bishops of today, keep silent when this confusion occurs.

This is what Pope Paul VI recommended in his opening discourse at the Medellin Conference: "Talk, speak out, preach, write. United in purpose and in programme, defend and explain the truths of the faith by taking a position on the present validity of the Gospel, on questions dealing with the life of the faithful and the defence of Christian conduct . . ." (Pope Paul VI's Discourse, I).

I too will not grow weary of repeating, as my duty of evangelizing the whole of mankind obliges me to do: "Do not be afraid. Open wide the doors for Christ. To his saving power open the boundaries of States, economic and political systems, the vast fields of culture, civilization and development" (the Pope's Homily at the Inauguration of the Pontificate, 22 October 1978).

I.6 You are teachers of the Truth, and you are expected to proclaim unceasingly, but with the special vigour at this moment, the truth concerning the mission of the Church, object of the Creed that we profess, and an indispensable and fundamental area of our fidelity. The Church was established by the Lord as a fellowship of life, love and truth (*Lumen Gentium,* 9) and as the body, the *Pleroma* and the sacrament of Christ, in whom the whole fullness of deity dwells (*Lumen Gentium,* 7).

The Church is born of our response in faith to Christ. In fact, it is by sincere acceptance of the Good News that we believers gather together in Jesus' name in order to seek together the Kingdom, build it up and live it (cf. *Evangelii Nuntiandi,* 13). The Church is "the assembly of those who in faith look to Jesus as the cause of salvation and the source of unity and peace" (*Lumen Gentium,* 9).

But on the other hand we are born of the Church. She communicates to us the riches of life and grace entrusted to her. She generates us by baptism, feeds us with the sacraments and the word of God, prepares us for mission, leads us to God's plan, the reason for our existence as Christians. We are her children. With just pride we call her our Mother, repeating a title coming down from the centuries, from the earliest times (cf. Henri de Lubac, *Meditation sur l'Eglise*).

She must therefore be called upon, respected and served, for "one cannot have God for his Father, if he does not have the Church for his Mother" (Saint Cyprian, *De Unitate,* 6, 8), one cannot love Christ without loving the Church which Christ loves (cf. *Evangelii Nuntiandi,* 16), and "to the extent that one loves the Church of Christ, he possesses the Holy Spirit" (Saint Augustine, *In Ioannem tract.,* 32, 8).

Love for the Church must be composed of fidelity and trust. Stressing, in the first discourse of my pontificate, my resolve to be faithful to the Second Vatican Council and my desire to dedicate my greatest care to the ecclesiological area, I called on people to take once again into their hands the Dogmatic Constitution *Lumen Gentium* in order to "meditate with renewed and invigorating zeal on the nature and function of the Church, her way of being and acting . . . not merely in order that the vital communion in Christ of all who believe and hope in him should be accomplished, but also in order to contribute to bringing about a fuller and closer unity of the whole human family" (First Message of John Paul II to the Church and the World, 17 October 1978).

Now, at this surpassing moment in the evangelization of Latin America, I repeat the call: "Assent to this document of the Council, seen in the light of Tradition and embodying the dogmatic formulae issued a century ago by the First Vatican Council, will be for us, pastors and faithful, a clear signpost and urgent incentive for walking—let us repeat—the paths of life and history" (*ibid.*).

I.7 There is no guarantee of serious and vigorous evangelizing activity without a well-founded ecclesiology.

The first reason is that evangelization is the essential mission, the distinctive vocation and the deepest identity of the Church, which has in turn been evangelized (*Evangelii Nuntiandi,* 14-15; *Lumen Gentium,* 5). She has been sent by the Lord and in her turn sends evangelizers to preach "not their own selves or their personal ideas, but a Gospel of which neither she nor they are the absolute masters and owners, to dispose of it as they wish" (*Evangelii Nuntiandi,* 15). A second reason is that evangelization is for no one an individual and isolated act; it is one that is deeply ecclesial (*Evangelii Nuntiandi,* 60), which is not subject to the discretionary power of individualistic criteria and perspectives but to that of communion with the Church and her pastors (cf. *ibid.*).

How could there be authentic evangelizing, if there were no ready and sincere reverence for the sacred Magisterium, in clear awareness that by submitting to it the People of God are not accepting the word of men but the true word of God? (cf. 1 *Thess.* 2:13; *Lumen Gentium,* 12). "The 'objective' importance of this Magisterium must always be kept in mind and also safeguarded, because of the attacks being levelled nowadays in various quarters against some certain truths of the Catholic faith" (First Message of John Paul II to the Church and the World, 17 October 1978).

I well know your attachment and availability to the See of Peter and the love that you have always shown it. From my heart I thank you in the Lord's name for the deeply ecclesial attitude implied in this and I wish you yourselves the consolation of counting on the loyal attachment of your faithful.

I.8 In the abundant documentation with which you have prepared this Conference, especially in the contributions of many Churches, a certain uneasiness is at times noticed with regard to the very interpretation of the nature and mission of the Church. Allusion is made, for instance, to the separation that some set up between the Church and the Kingdom of God. The Kingdom of God is emptied of its full content and is understood in a rather secularist sense: it is interpreted as being reached not by faith and membership in the Church but by the mere changing of structures and social and political involvement and activity for justice. This is to forget that "the Church receives the mission to proclaim and to establish among all peoples the Kingdom of Christ and of God. She becomes on earth the seed and beginning of that Kingdom" (*Lumen Gentium,* 5).

In one of his beautiful catechetical instructions Pope John Paul I, speaking of the virtue of hope, warned that "it is wrong to state that political, economic and social liberation coincides with salvation in Jesus Christ, that the *Regnum Dei* is identified with the *Regnum hominis*."

In some cases an attitude of mistrust is produced with regard to the "institutional" or "official" Church, which is considered as alienating, as opposed to another Church of the people, one springing from the people and taking concrete form in the poor. These positions could contain different, not always easily measured, degrees of familiar ideological forms of conditioning. The Council has reminded us what is the nature and mission of the Church. It has reminded us how her profound unity and permanent up-building are contributed to by those who are responsible for the ministry of the community and have to count on the collaboration of the whole People of God. In fact, "if the Gospel that we proclaim is seen to be rent by doctrinal disputes, ideological polarizations or mutual condemnations among Christians, at the mercy of the latter's differing views on Christ and the Church and even because of their different concepts of society and human institutions, how can those to whom we address our preaching fail to be disturbed, disoriented, even scandalized?" (*Evangelii Nuntiandi,* 77).

I.9 The truth that we owe to man is, first and foremost, a truth about man. As witnesses of Jesus Christ we are heralds, spokesmen and servants of this truth. We cannot reduce it to the principles of a system of philosophy or to pure political activity. We cannot forget it or betray it.

Perhaps one of the most obvious weaknesses of present-day civilization lies in an inadequate view of man. Without doubt, our age is the one in which man has been most written and spoken of, the age of the forms of humanism and the age of anthropocentrism. Nevertheless it is paradoxically also the age of man's abasement to previously unsuspected levels, the age of human values trampled on as never before.

How is this paradox explained? We can say that it is the inexorable paradox of atheistic humanism. It is the drama of man being deprived of an essential dimension of his being, namely, his search for the infinite, and thus faced with having his being reduced in the worst way. The Pastoral Constitution *Gaudium et Spes* plumbs the depths of the problem when it says: "Only in the mystery of the Incarnate Word does the mystery of man take on light" (*Gaudium et Spes,* 22).

Thanks to the Gospel, the Church has the truth about man. This truth is found in an anthropology that the Church never ceases to fathom more thoroughly and to communicate to others. The primordial affirmation of this anthropology is that man is God's image and cannot be reduced to a mere portion of nature or a nameless element in the human city (cf. *Gaudium et Spes,* 12 and 14). This is the meaning of what Saint Irenaeus wrote: "Man's glory is God, but the recipient of God's every action, of his wisdom and of his power is man" (Saint Irenaeus, *Adversus Haereses,* III, 20, 2-3).

I made particular reference to this irreplaceable foundation of the Christian concept of man in my Christmas Message: "Christmas is the feast of man . . . Man is an object to be counted, something considered under the aspect of quantity . . . Yet at the same time he is a single being, unique and unrepeatable . . . somebody thought of and chosen from eternity, someone called and identified by his own name" (Christmas Message, 1).

Faced with so many other forms of humanism that are often shut in by a strictly economic, biological or psychological view of man, the Church has the right and the duty to proclaim the Truth about man that she received from her teacher, Jesus Christ. God grant that no external compulsion may prevent her from doing so. God grant, above all, that she may not cease to do so through fear or doubt, through having let herself be contaminated by other forms of humanism, or through lack of confidence in her original message.

When a Pastor of the Church proclaims clearly and unambiguously the Truth about man that was revealed by him who "knew what was in man" (*Jn.* 2:25), he must therefore be encouraged by the certainty of doing the best service to the human being.

The complete truth about the human being constitutes the foundation of the Church's social teaching and the basis also of true liberation. In the light of this truth, man is not a being subjected to economic or political processes; these processes are instead directed to man and are subjected to him.

Without doubt, this truth about man that the Church teaches will go out strengthened from this meeting of Pastors.

Your pastoral service of truth is completed by a like service of unity.

II.1 *Unity among Bishops*

Unity will be, first of all, unity among yourselves, the Bishops. "We must guard and keep this unity," the Bishop Saint Cyprian wrote in a moment of grave threats to communion between the Bishops of his country, "especially we Bishops who preside over the Church, in order to give witness that the Episcopate is one and indivisible. Let no one mislead the faithful or alter the truth. The Episcopate is one" (*De Ecclesiae Catholicae Unitate,* 6-8).

This unity of Bishops comes not from human calculations and strategy but from on high: from serving one Lord, from being animated by one Spirit, and from loving one and the same Church. It is unity resulting from the mission that Christ has entrusted to us, the mission that has been evolving on the Latin American continent for almost half a millenium, and that you are carrying forward with stout hearts in times of profound changes as we approach the close of the second millennium of redemption and of the Church's activity. It is unity around the Gospel, the Body and Blood of the Lamb, and Peter living in his Successors; all of which are different signs, but all of them highly important signs, of the presence of Jesus among us.

What an occasion you have, dear Brothers, for living this unity of Pastors in this Conference! In itself it is a sign and result of an already existing unity; but it is also an anticipation and beginning of a unity that must be more and more close and solid. Begin your work in a climate of brotherly unity: even now let this unity be a component of evangelization.

II.2 *Unity with priests, religious and faithful*

Let unity among the Bishops be extended by unity with priests, religious and faithful. Priests are the immediate collaborators of the Bishops in their pastoral mission, and their mission would be compromised if close unity did not reign between priests and Bishops.

Men and women religious are also especially important subjects of that unity. I well know the importance of their contribution to evangelization in Latin America in the past and in the present. They came here at the dawn of the discovery and accompanied the first steps of almost all the countries. They worked continuously here together with the diocesan clergy. In some countries more than half, in other countries the great majority, of the body of priests are religious. This would be enough to show how important it is here more than in other parts of the world for religious not only to accept but to seek loyally an unbreakable unity of aim and action with their Bishops. To the Bishops the Lord entrusted the mission of feeding the flock. To religious it belongs to blaze the trails for evangelization. It cannot be, it ought not to be, that the Bishops should lack the responsible and active, yet at the same time, docile and trusting collaboration of the religious, whose charism makes them ever more ready agents at the service of the Gospel. In this matter everybody in the ecclesial community has the duty of avoiding magisteria other than the Church's Magisterium, for they are ecclesially unacceptable and pastorally sterile.

The laity also are subjects of that unity, whether involved individually or joined in apostolic associations for the spreading of the Kingdom of God. It is they who have to consecrate the world to Christ in the midst of their daily duties and in their various family and professional tasks, in close union with and obedience to the lawful Pastors.

In line with *Lumen Gentium,* we must safeguard the precious gift of ecclesial unity between all those who form part of the pilgrim People of God.

III.1 Those familiar with the Church's history know that in all periods there have been admirable Bishops deeply involved in advancing and valiantly defending the human dignity of those entrusted to them by the Lord. They have always been impelled to do so by their episcopal mission, because they considered human dignity a Gospel value that cannot be despised without greatly offending the Creator.

This dignity is infringed on the individual level when due regard is not had for values such as freedom, the right to profess one's religion, physical and mental integrity, the right to essential goods, to life . . . It is infringed on the social and political level when man cannot exercise his right of participation, or when he is subjected to unjust and unlawful coercion, or submitted to physical or mental torture, etc.

I am not unaware of how many questions are being posed in this sphere today in Latin America. As Bishops you cannot fail to concern yourselves with them. I know that you propose to carry out a serious reflection on the relationships and implications between evangelization and human advancement or liberation, taking into consideration, in such a vast and important field, what is specific about the Church's presence.

Here is where we find, brought concretely into practice, the themes we have touched upon in speaking of the truth concerning Christ, the Church and man.

III.2 If the Church makes herself present in the defence of, or in the advancement of, man, she does so in line with her mission, which, although it is religious and not social or political, cannot fail to consider man in the entirety of his being. The Lord outlined in the parable of the Good Samaritan the model of attention to all human needs (cf. *Lk.* 10:29ff.), and he said that in the final analysis he will identify himself with the disinherited—the sick, the imprisoned, the hungry, the lonely—who have been given a helping hand (*Mt.* 25:31ff.). The Church has learned in these and other pages of the Gospel (cf. *Mk.* 6:35-44) that the evangelizing mission has, as an essential part, action for justice and the tasks of the advancement of man (cf. final document of the Synod of Bishops, October 1971), and that between evangelization and human advancement there are very strong links of the orders of anthropology, theology and love (cf. *Evangelii Nuntiandi,* 31); so that "evangelization would not be complete if it did not take into account the unceasing interplay of the Gospel and of man's concrete life, both personal and social" (*Evangelii Nuntiandi,* 29).

Let us also keep in mind that the Church's action in earthly matters such as human advancement, development, justice, the rights of the individual, is always intended to be at the service of man; and of man as she sees him in the Christian vision of the anthropology that she adopts. She therefore does not need to have recourse to ideological systems in order to love, defend and collaborate in the liberation of man: at the centre of the message of which she is the depository and herald she finds inspiration for acting in favour of brotherhood, justice, and peace, against all forms of domination, slavery, discrimination, violence, attacks on religious liberty and aggression against man, and whatever attacks life (cf. *Gaudium et Spes,* 26, 27 and 29).

III.3 It is therefore not through opportunism nor thirst for novelty that the Church, "the expert in humanity" (Paul VI, Address to the United Nations, 4 October 1965) defends human rights. It is through a true *evangelical commitment,* which, as happened with Christ, is a commitment to the most needy. In fidelity to this commitment, the Church wishes to stay free with regard to the competing systems, in order to opt only for man. Whatever the miseries or sufferings that afflict man, it is not through violence, the interplay of power and political systems, but through the truth concerning man, that he journeys towards a better future.

III.4 Hence the Church's constant preoccupation with the delicate question of property. A proof of this is the writings of the Fathers of the Church through the first thousand years of Christianity (cf. St Ambrose, *De Nabuthe,* c. 12, n. 53: *PL* 14, 747). It is clearly shown by the vigorous teaching of Saint Thomas Aquinas, repeated so many times. In our own times, the Church has appealed to the same principles in such far-reaching documents as the social Encyclicals of the recent Popes. With special force and profundity, Pope Paul VI spoke of this subject in his Encyclical *Populorum Progressio* (cf. nos. 23-24; cf. also *Mater et Magistra,* 1.06).

This voice of the Church, echoing the voice of human conscience, and which did not cease to make itself heard down the centuries in the midst of the most varied social and cultural systems and conditions, deserves and needs to be heard in our time also, when the growing wealth of a few parallels the growing poverty of the masses.

It is then that the Church's teaching, according to which all private property involves a social obligation, acquires an urgent character. With respect to this teaching, the Church has a mission to carry out; she must preach, educate individuals and collectivities, form public opinion, and offer orientations to the leaders of the peoples. In this way she will be working in favour of society, within which this Christian and evangelical principle will finally bear the fruit of a more just and equitable distribution of goods, not only within each nation but also in the world in general, ensuring that the stronger countries do not use their power to the detriment of the weaker ones.

Those who bear responsibility for the public life of the States and nations will have to understand that internal peace and international peace can only be ensured if a social and economic system based on justice flourishes.

Christ did not remain indifferent in the face of this vast and demanding imperative of social morality. Nor could the Church. In the spirit of the Church, which is the spirit of Christ, and relying upon her ample and solid doctrine, let us return to work in this field.

It must be emphasized here once more that the Church's solicitude looks to the whole man.

For this reason, for an economic system to be just it is an indispensable condition that it should favour the development and diffusion of public education and culture. The more just the economy, the deeper will be the conscience of culture. This is very much in line with what the Council stated: that to attain a life worthy of man, it is not possible to limit oneself to *having more;* one must aspire to *being more* (cf. *Gaudium et Spes,* 35).

Therefore, Brothers, drink at these authentic fountains. Speak with the language of the Council, of John XXIII, of Paul VI: it is the language of the experience, of the suffering, of the hope of modern humanity.

When Paul VI declared that development is "the new name of peace" (*Populorum Progressio,* 76), he had in mind all the links of interdependence that exist not only within the nations but also those outside them, on the world level. He took into consideration the mechanisms that, because they happen to be imbued not with authentic humanism but with materialism, produce on the international level rich people ever more rich at the expense of poor people ever more poor.

There is no economic rule capable of changing these mechanisms by itself. It is necessary, in international life, to call upon ethical principles, the demands of justice, the primary commandment which is that of love. Primacy must be given to what is moral, to what is spiritual, to what springs from the full truth concerning man.

I have wished to manifest to you these reflections which I consider very important, although they must not distract you from the central theme of the Conference: we shall reach man, we shall reach justice, through evangelization.

III.5 In the face of what has been said hitherto, the Church sees with deep sorrow "the sometimes massive increase of human rights violations in all parts of society and of the world . . . Who can deny that today individual persons and civil powers violate basic rights of the human person with impunity: rights such as the right to be born, the right to life, the right to responsible procreation, to work, to peace, to freedom and social justice, the right to participate in the decisions that affect people and nations? And what can be said when we face the various forms of collective violence like discrimination against individuals and groups, the use of physical and psychological torture perpetrated against prisoners or political dissenters? The list grows when we turn to the instances of the abduction of persons for political reasons and look at the acts of kidnapping for material gain which attack so dramatically family life and the social fabric" (Message of John Paul II to the Secretary-General of the United Nations Organization on 2 December 1978: 30th Anniversary of the Declaration of Human Rights). We cry out once more: Respect man! He is the image of God! Evangelize, so that this may become a reality; so that the Lord may transform hearts and humanize the political and economic systems, with man's responsible commitment as the starting point!

III.6 Pastoral commitments in this field must be encouraged through a correct Christian idea of liberation. The Church feels the duty to proclaim the liberation of millions of human beings, the duty to help this liberation become firmly established (cf. *Evangelii Nuntiandi,* 30); but she also feels the corresponding duty to proclaim liberation in its integral and profound meaning, as Jesus proclaimed and realized it (cf. *Evangelii Nuntiandi,* 31). "Liberation from everything that oppresses man but which is, above all, liberation from sin and the Evil One, in the joy of knowing God and being known by him" (*Evangelii Nuntiandi,* 9). Liberation made up of reconciliation and forgiveness. Liberation springing from the reality of being children of God, whom we are able to call Abba, Father (*Rom.* 8:15); a reality which makes us recognize in every man a brother of ours, capable of being transformed in his heart through God's mercy. Liberation that, with the energy of love, urges us towards fellowship, the summit and fullness of which we find in the Lord. Liberation as the overcoming of the various forms of slavery and man-made idols, and as the growth of the new man. Liberation that in the framework of the Church's proper mission is not reduced to the simple and narrow economic, political, social or cultural dimension, and is not sacrificed to the demands of any strategy, practice or short-term solution (cf. *Evangelii Nuntiandi,* 33).

To safeguard the originality of Christian liberation and the energies that it is capable of releasing, one must at all costs avoid any form of curtailment or ambiguity, as Pope Paul VI asked: "The Church would lose her fundamental meaning. Her message of liberation would no longer have any originality and would easily be open to monopolization and manipulation by ideological systems and political parties" (*Evangelii Nuntiandi,* 32). There are many signs that help to distinguish when the liberation in question is Christian and when on the other hand it is based rather on ideologies that rob it of consistency with an evangelical view of man, of things and of events (cf. *Evangelii Nuntiandi,* 35). They are signs drawn from the content of what the evangelizers proclaim or from the concrete attitudes that they adopt. At the level of content, one must see what is their fidelity to the word of God, to the Church's living Tradition and to her Magisterium. As for attitudes, one must consider what sense of communion they have with the Bishops, in the first place, and with the other sectors of the People of God; what contribution they make to the real building up of the community; in what form they lovingly show care for the poor, the sick, the dispossessed, the neglected and the oppressed, and in what way they find in them the image of the poor and suffering Jesus, and strive to relieve their need and serve Christ in them (cf. *Lumen Gentium,* 8). Let us not deceive ourselves: the humble and simple faithful, as though by an evangelical instinct, spontaneously sense when the Gospel is served in the Church and when it is emptied of its content and is stifled with other interests.

As you see, the series of observations made by *Evangelii Nuntiandi* on the theme of liberation retains all its validity.

III.7 What we have already recalled constitutes a rich and complex heritage, which *Evangelii Nuntiandi* calls the Social Doctrine or Social Teaching of the Church (cf. *Evangelii Nuntiandi* 38). This teaching comes into being, in the light of the Word of God and the authentic Magisterium, from the presence of Christians in the midst of the changing situations of the world, in contact with the challenges that result from those situations. This social doctrine involves therefore both principles for reflection and also norms for judgment and guidelines for action (cf. *Octogesima Adveniens,* 4).

Placing responsible confidence in this social doctrine—even though some people seek to sow doubts and lack of confidence in it—to give it serious study, to try to apply it, to teach it, to be faithful to it: all this is the guarantee, in a member of the Church, of his commitment in the delicate and demanding social tasks, and of his efforts in favour of the liberation or advancement of his brothers and sisters.

Allow me therefore to recommend to your special pastoral attention the urgent need to make your faithful people aware of this social doctrine of the Church.

Particular care must be given to forming a social conscience at all levels and in all sectors. When injustices grow worse and the distance between rich and poor increases distressingly, the social doctrine, in a form which is creative and open to the broad fields of the Church's presence, must be a valuable instrument for formation and action. This holds good particularly for the laity: "it is the laity, though not exclusively to them, that secular duties and activity properly belong" (*Gaudium et Spes,* 43). It is necessary to avoid supplanting the laity and to study seriously just when certain forms of supplying for them retain their reason for existence. Is it not the laity who are called, by reason of their vocation in the Church, to make their contribution in the political and economic dimensions, and to be effectively present in the safeguarding and advancement of human rights?

You are going to consider many pastoral themes of great significance. Time prevents me from mentioning them. Some I have referred to or will do so in the meetings with the priests, religious, seminarians, and lay people.

IV.1 The themes that I indicate here have, for different reasons, great importance. You will not fail to consider them, among the many others that your pastoral farsightedness will indicate to you.

a) The Family: Make every effort to ensure that there is pastoral care for the family. Attend to this field of such primary importance in the certainty that evangelization in the future depends largely on the "domestic Church." It is the school of love, of the knowledge of God, of respect for life and for human dignity. The importance of this pastoral care is in proportion to the threats aimed at the family. Think of the campaigns in favour of divorce, of the use of contraceptive practices, and of abortion, which destroy society.

b) Priestly and religious vocations: In the majority of your countries, in spite of an encouraging awakening of vocations, the lack of vocations is a grave and chronic problem. There is a huge disproportion between the growing population and the number of agents of evangelization. This is of great importance to the Christian community. Every community has to obtain its vocations, as a sign of its vitality and maturity. Intense pastoral activity must be reactivated, starting with the Christian vocation in general and from enthusiastic pastoral care for youth, so as to give the Church the ministers she needs. Lay vocations, although they are so indispensable, cannot compensate for them. Furthermore, one of the proofs of the laity's commitment is an abundance of vocations to the consecrated life.

c) Youth: How much hope the Church places in youth! How much energy needed by the Church abounds in youth, in Latin America! How close we Pastors must be to the young, so that Christ and the Church and love of the brethren may penetrate deeply into their hearts.

At the end of this message I cannot fail to invoke once again the protection of the Mother of God upon your persons and your work during these days. The fact that this meeting of ours is taking place in the spiritual presence of Our Lady of Guadalupe, who is venerated in Mexico and in all the other countries as the Mother of the Church in Latin America, is for me a cause of joy and a source of hope. May she, the "Star of evangelization," be your guide in your future reflections and decisions. May she obtain for you from her Divine Son:

— the boldness of prophets and the evangelical prudence of Pastors,

— the clearsightedness of teachers and the reliability of guides and directors,

— courage as witnesses, and the calmness, patience and gentleness of fathers.

May the Lord bless your labours. You are accompanied by select representatives: priests, deacons, men and women religious, lay people, experts and observers, whose collaboration will be very useful to you. The whole Church has its eyes on you, with confidence and hope. You intend to respond to these expectations with full fidelity to Christ, the Church, and humanity. The future is in God's hands, but in a certain way God places that future with new evangelizing momentum in your hands too. "Go therefore and make disciples of all nations" (*Mt.* 28:19).

Christian Marriage

Address of His Holiness John Paul II to the Second General Assembly of the Pontifical Council for the Family (May 26, 1984)

Dear Brothers and Sisters,

1. I am most pleased to meet with you, Members of the Pontifical Council for the Family, as friends and collaborators in a field which is so important for the life of the Church and society. In fact, to a great extent, both the civil and religious future of humanity depend on the family because on it depends the very well-being of the human person. I am, therefore, most grateful to you for the collaboration provided in promoting pastoral care of the family which represents an important means of evangelization and an area which has always been particularly dear to me in my ministry in the Archdiocese of Krakow and continues to be so today in my apostolic care.

2. The theme that has concerned you in this General Assembly, in the light of a careful analysis of the various situations in the local Churches, is "Preparation for Christian Marriage."

It is a theme of the greatest importance and urgency. Many times I have expressed my personal conviction that "the future of humanity passes by way of the family" (cf. *Familiaris Consortio,* 86). It is possible, however, to go further and state that *the future of the family passes by way of its adequate preparation.* Here we are touching on a value and a need which concerns not only the young people called to marriage, but the entire ecclesial and civil community as well. Just think of the riches which the Church, and not only, can receive from those preparing to marry: the freshness and enthusiasm of love, the taste for beauty, the desire for an open dialogue, and the hope for tomorrow are a gift for everyone and a reminder to those who are already married, almost an invitation to return to the source of their choice, to the "springtime" of their love.

3. The Apostolic Exhortation "Familiaris Consortio" treats the theme of marriage preparation explicitly and broadly in its various stages—remote, proximate, immediate—and emphasizes the importance the family has in preparing children for the Sacrament of Matrimony. It is in the family that the first and deepest foundations are set of the psy-

chological and moral attitudes that will make married life possible by readying future partners to take on the responsibilities which the Sacrament of Matrimony brings. Your responses to the questionnaire, sent to you during the preparatory period of the Assembly, confirm this conviction and emphasize that the best remote preparation for children's future marriage is an exemplary Christian family life in which the witness provided by spouses is essential. The family environment, enlightened by parents' proper teaching, represents children's best preparation for life and thus also for marriage.

4. As they grow, children later enter into a particularly important, delicate and difficult period of their education. The need to win their own identity leads adolescents to a form of self-assertion which often includes the temptation to assume an attitude of contestation of their parents' authority and to take a certain distance from the family environment which had been, up until that time, almost the sole environment of their lives. Precisely at this time, the fascinating discovery of the opposite sex takes place, and the influence of elements from outside the family in the adolescent's life is accentuated, especially from the mass media, peer pressure, the school. All of this makes more difficult, but not for this reason less important, parents' educational activity which at this point is expressed above all in the guiding force of the example and discrete influence of a prudent attitude that cultivates a deep bond with the young person suitable in form and style to his or her age and personal characteristics.

By dedicating sufficient time and attention to him or her, parents can make the young person aware of how much they love him or her in a way which is faithful, tenacious and respectful of his or her personality and freedom and always ready to help and receive, especially in times of need.

5. During adolescence, other elements from outside the family intervene with special vigor, as has been said, and influence the development of young people. I particularly refer to the school and to the means of social communication. In both areas, the Pontifical Council for the Family must work on initiatives aimed at helping families effectively in the essential task of educating their children, especially with regard to education for love.

A much closer coordination and cooperation must be fostered and achieved between parents and educators in schools. Parents cannot delegate all their educational functions to schools which, on their part, cannot separate themselves from the parents who have entrusted their children to them for a complete education. The school and parents must help one another reciprocally in the educational task of the child and adolescent, also concerning education for love and marriage. But we cannot forget that many boys and girls attend non-Catholic schools where they often do not receive proper guidance in this area, or they receive instruction or experience an environment which does not help them form a Christian vision of love, sexuality and marriage. Parents' duty in this case becomes even more serious both with regard to the school and, above all, to the environment of one's own family where they must carry out an educational activity and offer witness capable of contrasting and overcoming the negative influences which the teaching or environment have on their children.

6. The means of social communication merit special mention. From your replies to the questionnaire, the great influence these means have appears very clearly and that it is generally negative. The Pontifical Council for the Family has here another important area for action both for identifying the means to help parents use wisely and with critical judgment the means of social communication, as well as to encourage initiatives by artists and the various agents of the mass media to offer more programs more positively inspired by Christian values. The mass media have a great influence in our modern culture and it is not possible to overlook them. Therefore it is necessary to commit oneself to utilizing them with their enormous potential for the good of persons and families without letting oneself become conditioned by interests which frequently make us forget the true moral well-being of children, young people and families to whom they are directed.

7. When there is good remote and proximate preparation for marriage, immediate preparation becomes easier and richer. The many efforts made in this latter area have increased awareness in the Church that for Matrimony, as for every other sacrament, there must be adequate preparation in order for the celebration to be rich in the life of the spouses.

The new Code of Canon Law has included marriage preparation among the duties of the ecclesial community (cf. CIC 1063), and especially of pastors.

8. Preparation for marriage opens up vast fields of action to the Pontifical Council for the Family which must be tackled with enthusiasm, creativity, energy and constancy.

One must not become discouraged in the face of the difficulties which will inevitably be encountered. No sacrifice can refrain the Christian community and single families from the very essential task of preparing well future spouses who will make up the families of the third millenium of Christian life. Furthermore, no initiative should be put aside which may be helpful to already existing families who wish to know, understand and realize their duty better in those difficult situations in which they are frequently called to live.

I ask you to place all your efforts in being close to these families, to support them in every way and educate them to the love that, in the Sacrament of Matrimony, through the free gift of Jesus Christ, becomes the imitation and participation of the Lord's love for his Church.

In expressing my appreciation for your generous dedication, with great affection I impart my Apostolic Blessing to you, your families and all those who are the object of your attention and pastoral action.

Cultivating Peace on Earth

At the General Assembly of the United Nations on 2 October 1979, John Paul II delivered his appeal for peace and human rights to the representatives of 151 nations, and through them to all the inhabitants of the earth. After addresses of welcome by Mr. Salim Ahmed Salim, President of the General Assembly, and Dr. Kurt Waldheim, Secretary General of the United Nations, Pope John Paul delivered the following address:

Mr. President,

1. I desire to express my gratitude to the General Assembly of the United Nations, which I am permitted today to participate in and to address. My thanks go in the first place to the Secretary General of the United Nations Organization, Dr. Kurt Waldheim. Last autumn, soon after my election to the Chair of Saint Peter, he invited me to make this visit, and he renewed his invitation in the course of our meeting in Rome last May. From the first moment I felt greatly honoured and deeply obliged. And today, before this distinguished Assembly, I also thank you, Mr. President, who have so kindly welcomed me and invited me to speak.

2. The formal reason for my intervention today is, without any question, the special bond of cooperation that links the Apostolic See with the United Nations Organization, as is shown by the presence of the Holy See's Permanent Observer to this Organization. The existence of this bond, which is held in high esteem by the Holy See, rests on the sovereignty with which the Apostolic See has been endowed for many centuries. The territorial extent of that sovereignty is limited to the small State of Vatican City, but the sovereignty itself is warranted by the need of the papacy to exercise its mission in full freedom, and to be able to deal with any interlocutor, whether a government or an international organization, without dependence on other sovereignties. Of course the nature and aims of the spiritual mission of the Apostolic See and the Church make their participation in the tasks and activities of the United Nations Organization very different from that of the States, which are communities in the political and temporal sense.

3. Besides attaching great importance to its collaboration with the United Nations Organization, the Apostolic See has always, since the foundation of your Organization, expressed its esteem and its agreement

with the historic significance of this supreme forum for the international life of humanity today. It also never ceases to support your Organization's functions and initiatives, which are aimed at peaceful coexistence and collaboration between nations. There are many proofs of this. In the more than thirty years of the existence of the United Nations Organization, it has received much attention in papal messages and encyclicals, in documents of the Catholic episcopate, and likewise in the Second Vatican Council. Pope John XXIII and Pope Paul VI looked with confidence on your important institution as an eloquent and promising sign of our times. He who is now addressing you has, since the first months of his pontificate, several times expressed the same confidence and conviction as his predecessors.

4. This confidence and conviction on the part of the Apostolic See is the result, as I have said, not of merely political reasons but of the religious and moral character of the mission of the Roman Catholic Church. As a universal community embracing faithful belonging to almost all countries and continents, nations, peoples, races, languages and cultures, the Church is deeply interested in the existence and activity of the Organization whose very name tells us that it unites and associates nations and States. It unites and associates: it does not divide and oppose. It seeks out the ways for understanding and peaceful collaboration, and endeavours with the means at its disposal and the methods in its power to exclude war, division and mutual destruction within the great family of humanity today.

5. This is the real reason, the essential reason, for my presence among you, and I wish to thank this distinguished Assembly for giving consideration to this reason, which can make my presence among you in some way useful. It is certainly a highly significant fact that among the representatives of the States, whose raison d'etre is the sovereignty of powers linked with territory and people, there is also today the representative of the Apostolic See and the Catholic Church. This Church is the Church of Jesus Christ, who declared before the tribunal of the Roman judge Pilate that he was a king, but with a kingdom not of this world (cf. *Jn.* 18:36-37). When he was then asked about the reason for the existence of his kingdom among men, he explained: "For this I was born, and for this I have come into the world, to bear witness to the truth" (*Jn.* 18:37). Here, before the representatives of the States, I wish not only to thank you but also to offer my special congratulations, since the invitation extended to the Pope to speak in your Assembly shows that the United Nations Organization accepts and respects the religious and moral dimension of those human problems that the Church attends to, in view of the message of truth and love that it is her duty to bring to the world. The questions that

concern your functions and receive your attention—as is indicated by the vast organic complex of institutions and activities that are part of or collaborate with the United Nations, especially in the fields of culture, health, food, labour, and the peaceful uses of nuclear energy—certainly make it essential for us to meet in the name of man in his wholeness, in all the fullness and manifold riches of his spiritual and material existence, as I have stated in my encyclical *Redemptor Hominis,* the first of my pontificate.

6. Now, availing myself of the solemn occasion of my greeting with the representatives of the nations of the earth, I wish above all to send my greetings to all the men and women living on this planet. To every man and every woman, without any exception whatever. Every human being living on earth is a member of a civil society, of a nation, many of them represented here. Each one of you, distinguished ladies and gentlemen, represents a particular State, system and political structure, but what you represent above all are individual human beings; you are all representatives of men and women, of practically all the people of the world, individual men and women, communities and peoples who are living the present phase of their own history and who are also part of the history of humanity as a whole, each of them a subject endowed with dignity as a human person, with his or her own culture, experiences and aspirations, tensions and sufferings, and legitimate expectations. This relationship is what provides the reason for all political activity, whether national or international, for in the final analysis this activity comes *from man,* is exercised *by man* and is *for man.* And if political activity is cut off from this fundamental relationship and finality, if it becomes in a way its own end, it loses much of its reason to exist. Even more, it can also give rise to a specific alienation; it can become extraneous to man; it can come to contradict humanity itself. In reality, what justifies the existence of any political activity is service to man, concerned and responsible attention to the essential problems and duties of his earthly existence in its social dimension and significance, on which also the good of each person depends.

7. I ask you, ladies and gentlemen, to excuse me for speaking of questions that are certainly self-evident for you. But it does not seem pointless to speak of them, since the most frequent pitfall for human activities is the possibility of losing sight, while performing them, of the clearest truths, the most elementary principles.

I would like to express the wish that, in view of its universal character, the United Nations Organization will never cease to be the forum, the high tribune from which all man's problems are appraised in truth and justice. It was in the name of this inspiration, it was through this historic stimulus, that on 26 June 1945, towards the end of the terrible Second World War, the Charter of the United Nations was signed and on the following 24 October your Organization began its life. Soon after, on 10 December 1948, came its fundamental document, the *Universal Declaration of Human Rights,* the rights of the human being as a concrete individual and of the human being in his universal value. This document is a milestone on the long and difficult path of the human race. The progress of humanity must be measured not only by the progress of science and technology, which shows man's uniqueness with regard to nature, but also and chiefly by the primacy given to spiritual values and by the progress of moral life. In this field is manifested the full dominion of reason, through truth, in the behaviour of the individual and of society, and also the control of reason over nature; and thus human conscience quietly triumphs, as was expressed in the ancient saying: *"Genus humanum arte et ratione vivit."*

It was when technology was being directed in its one-sided progress towards goals of war, hegemony and conquest, so that man might kill man and nation destroy nation by depriving it of its liberty and the right to exist—and I still have before my mind the image of the Second World War in Europe, which began forty years ago on 1 September 1939 with the invasion of Poland and ended on 9 May 1945—it was precisely then that the United Nations Organization arose. And three years later the document appeared which, as I have said, must be considered a real milestone on the path of the moral progress of humanity—the *Universal Declaration of Human Rights.* The governments and States of the world have understood that, if they are not to attack and destroy each other, they must unite. The real way, the fundamental way to this is through each human being, through the definition and recognition of and respect for the inalienable rights of individuals and of the communities of peoples.

8. Today, forty years after the outbreak of the Second World War, I wish to recall the whole of the experiences by individuals and nations that were sustained by a generation that is largely still alive. I had occasion not long ago to reflect again on some of those experiences, in one of the places that are most distressing and overflowing with contempt for man and his fundamental rights—the extermination camp of Oswiecim (Auschwitz), which I visited during my pilgrimage to Poland last June. This infamous place is unfortunately only one of the many scattered over the continent of Europe. But the memory of even one should be a warning sign on the path of humanity today, in order that every kind of concentration camp anywhere on earth may once and for all be done away with. And everything that recalls those horrible experiences should also

disappear forever from the lives of nations and States, everything that is a continuation of those experiences under different forms, namely the various kinds of torture and oppression, either physical or moral, carried out under any system, in any land; this phenomenon is all the more distressing if it occurs under the pretext of internal "security" or the need to preserve an apparent peace.

9. You will forgive me, ladies and gentlemen, for evoking this memory. But I would be untrue to the history of this century, I would be dishonest with regard to the great cause of man, which we all wish to serve, if I should keep silent, I who come from the country on whose living body Oswiecim was at one time constructed. But my purpose in evoking this memory is above all to show what painful experiences and sufferings by millions of people gave rise to the *Universal Declaration of Human Rights,* which has been placed as the basic inspiration and cornerstone of the United Nations Organization. This Declaration was paid for by millions of our brothers and sisters at the cost of their suffering and sacrifice, brought about by the brutalization that darkened and made insensitive the human consciences of their oppressors and of those who carried out a real genocide. This price cannot have been paid in vain! The *Universal Declaration of Human Rights*—with its train of many declarations and conventions on highly important aspects of human rights, in favour of children, of women, of equality between races, and especially the two international covenants on economic, social and cultural rights and on civil and political rights—must remain the basic value in the United Nations Organization with which the consciences of its members must be confronted and from which they must draw continual inspiration. If the truths and principles contained in this document were to be forgotten or ignored and were thus to lose the genuine self-evidence that distinguished them at the time they were brought painfully to birth, then the noble purpose of the United Nations Organization could be faced with the threat of a new destruction. This is what would happen if the simple yet powerful eloquence of the *Universal Declaration of Human Rights* were decisively subjugated by what is wrongly called political interest, but often really means no more than one-sided gain and advantage to the detriment of others, or a thirst for power regardless of the needs of others—everything which by its nature is opposed to the spirit of the Declaration. "Political interest" understood in this sense, if you will pardon me, ladies and gentlemen, dishonours the noble and difficult mission of your service for the good of your countries and of all humanity.

10. Fourteen years ago my great predecessor Pope Paul VI spoke from this podium. He spoke memorable words, which I desire to repeat today:

"No more war, war never again! Never one against the other," or even "one above the other," but always, on every occasion, "with each other."

Paul VI was a tireless servant of the cause of peace. I wish to follow him with all my strength and continue his service. The Catholic Church in every place on earth proclaims a message of peace, prays for peace, educates for peace. This purpose is also shared by the representatives and followers of other Churches and Communities and of other religions of the world, and they have pledged themselves to it. In union with efforts by all people of good will, this work is certainly bearing fruit. Nevertheless we are continually troubled by the armed conflicts that break out from time to time. How grateful we are to the Lord when a direct intervention succeeds in avoiding such a conflict, as in the case of the tension that last year threatened Argentina and Chile.

It is my fervent hope that a solution also to the Middle East crises may draw nearer. While being prepared to recognize the value of any concrete step or attempt made to settle the conflict, I want to recall that it would have no value if it did not truly represent the "first stone" of a general overall peace in the area, a peace that, being necessarily based on equitable recognition of the rights of all, cannot fail to include the consideration and just settlement of the Palestinian question. Connected with this question is that of the tranquility, independence, and territorial integrity of Lebanon within the formula that has made it an example of peaceful and mutually fruitful coexistence between distinct communities, a formula that I hope will, in the common interest, be maintained, with the adjustments required by the developments of the situation. I also hope for a special statute that, under international guarantees—as my predecessor Paul VI indicated—would respect the particular nature of Jerusalem, a heritage sacred to the veneration of millions of believers of the three great monotheistic religions, Judaism, Christianity and Islam.

We are troubled also by reports of the development of weaponry exceeding in quality and size the means of war and destruction ever known before. In this field also we applaud the decisions and agreements aimed at reducing the arms race. Nevertheless, the life of humanity today is seriously endangered by the threat of destruction and by the risk arising even from accepting certain "tranquillizing" reports. And the resistance to actual concrete proposals of real disarmament, such as those called for by this Assembly in a special session last year, shows that together with the will for peace that all profess and that most desire there is also in existence—perhaps in latent or conditional form but nonetheless real—the contrary and the negation of this will. The continual preparations for war demonstrated by the production of ever more numerous, powerful and sophisticated weapons in various countries show that there is a desire to be ready for war, and being ready means being able to start it; it also means taking the risk that sometime, somewhere, somehow, someone can set in motion the terrible mechanism of general destruction.

11. It is therefore necessary to make a continuing and even more energetic effort to do away with the very possibility of provoking war, and to make such catastrophes impossible by influencing the attitudes and convictions, the very intentions and aspirations of governments and peoples. This duty, kept constantly in mind by the United Nations Organization and each of its institutions, must also be a duty for every society, every regime, every government. This task is certainly served by initiatives aimed at international cooperation for the fostering of development. As Paul VI said at the end of his encyclical *Populorum Progressio,* "If the new name for peace is development, who would not wish to labour for it with all his powers?" However, this task must be also be served by constant reflection and activity aimed at discovering the very roots of hatred, destructiveness and contempt—the roots of everything that produces the temptation to war, not so much in the hearts of the nations as in the inner determination of the systems that decide the history of whole societies. In this titanic labour of building up the peaceful future of our planet the United Nations Organization has undoubtedly a key function and guiding role, for which it must refer to the just ideals contained in the Universal Declaration of Human Rights. For this Declaration has struck a real blow against the many deep roots of war, since the spirit of war, in its basic primordial meaning, springs up and grows to maturity where the inalienable rights of man are violated.

This is a new and deeply relevant vision of the cause of peace, one that goes deeper and is more radical. It is a vision that sees the genesis, and in a sense the substance, of war in the more complex forms emanating from injustice viewed in all its various aspects: this injustice first attacks human rights and thereby destroys the organic unity of the social order and it then affects the whole system of international relations. Within the Church's doctrine, the encyclical *Pacem in Terris* by John XXIII provides in synthetic form a view of this matter that is very close to the ideological foundation of the United Nations Organization. This must therefore form the basis to which one must loyally and perseveringly adhere in order to establish true "peace on earth."

12. By applying this criterion we must diligently examine which principal tensions in connection with the inalienable rights of man can weaken the construction of this peace which we all desire so ardently and which is the essential goal of the efforts of the United Nations Organization. It is not easy, but it must be done. Anyone who undertakes it must

take up a totally objective position and be guided by sincerity, readiness to acknowledge one's prejudices and mistakes and readiness even to renounce one's own particular interests, including political interests. Peace is something greater and more important than any of these interests. It is by sacrificing these interests for the sake of peace that we serve them best. After all, in whose "political interest" can it ever be to have another war?

Every analysis must necessarily start from the premise that—although each person lives in a particular concrete social and historical context—every human being is endowed with a dignity that must never be lessened, impaired or destroyed but must instead be respected and safeguarded, if peace is really to be built up.

13. In a movement that one hopes will be progressive and continuous, the *Universal Declaration of Human Rights* and the other international and national juridical instruments are endeavouring to create general awareness of the dignity of the human being, and to define at least some of the inalienable rights of man. Permit me to enumerate some of the most important human rights that are universally recognized: the right to life, liberty and security of person; the right to food, clothing, housing, sufficient health care, rest and leisure; the right to freedom of expression, education and culture; the right to freedom of thought, conscience and religion, and the right to manifest one's religion either individually or in community, in public or in private; the right to choose a state of life, to found a family and to enjoy all conditions necessary for family life; the right to property and work, to adequate working conditions and a just wage; the right of assembly and association; the right to freedom of movement, to internal and external migration; the right to nationality and residence; the right to political participation and the right to participate in the free choice of the political system of the people to which one belongs. All these human rights taken together are in keeping with the substance of the dignity of the human being, understood in his entirety, not as reduced to one dimension only. These rights concern the satisfaction of man's essential needs, the exercise of his freedoms, and his relationships with others; but always and everywhere they concern man, they concern man's full human dimension.

14. Man lives at the same time both in the world of material values and in that of spiritual values. For the individual living and hoping man, his needs, freedoms and relationships with others never concern one sphere of values alone, but belong to both. Material and spiritual realities may be viewed separately in order to understand better that in the concrete human being they are inseparable, and to see that any threat to human rights, whether in the field of material realities or in that of spir-

itual realities, is equally dangerous for peace, since in every instance it concerns man in his entirety. Permit me, distinguished ladies and gentlemen, to recall a constant rule of the history of humanity, a rule that is implicitly contained in all that I have already stated with regard to integral development and human rights. The rule is based on the relationship between spiritual values and material or economic values. In this relationship, it is the spiritual values that are pre-eminent, both on account of the nature of these values and also for reasons concerning the good of man. The pre-eminence of the values of the spirit defines the proper sense of earthly material goods and the way to use them. This pre-eminence is therefore at the basis of a just peace. It is also a contributing factor to ensuring that material development, technical development and the development of civilization are at the service of what constitutes man. This means enabling man to have full access to truth, to moral development, and to the complete possibility of enjoying the goods of culture which he has inherited, and of increasing them by his own creativity. It is easy to see that material goods do not have unlimited capacity for satisfying the needs of man: they are not in themselves easily distributed and, in the relationship between those who possess and enjoy them and those who are without them, they give rise to tension, dissension and division that will often even turn into open conflict. Spiritual goods, on the other hand, are open to unlimited enjoyment by many at the same time, without diminution of the goods themselves. Indeed, the more people share in such goods, the more they are enjoyed and drawn upon, the more then do those goods show their indestructible and immortal worth. This truth is confirmed, for example, by the works of creativity—I mean by the works of thought, poetry, music, and the figurative arts, fruits of man's spirit.

15. A critical analysis of our modern civilization shows that in the last hundred years it has contributed as never before to the development of material goods, but that it has also given rise, both in theory and still more in practice, to a series of attitudes in which sensitivity to the spiritual dimension of human existence is diminished to a greater or less extent, as a result of certain premises which reduce the meaning of human life chiefly to the many different material and economic factors—I mean to the demands of production, the market, consumption, the accumulation of riches or of the growing bureaucracy with which an attempt is made to regulate these very processes. Is this not the result of having subordinated man to one single conception and sphere of values?

16. What is the link between these reflections and the cause of peace and war? Since, as I have already stated, material goods by their very nature provoke conditionings and divisions, the struggle to obtain these

goods becomes inevitable in the history of humanity. If we cultivate this one-sided subordination of man to material goods alone, we shall be incapable of overcoming this state of need. We shall be able to attenuate it and avoid it in particular cases, but we shall not succeed in eliminating it systematically and radically, unless we emphasize more and pay greater honour, before everyone's eyes, in the sight of every society, to the second dimension of the goods of man: the dimension that does not divide people but puts them into communication with each other, associates them and unites them.

I consider that the famous opening words of the Charter of the United Nations, in which "the peoples of the United Nations, determined to save succeeding generations from the scourge of war" solemnly reaffirmed "faith in fundamental human rights, in the dignity and worth of the human person, in the equal rights of men and women and of nations large and small," are meant to stress this dimension.

Indeed, the fight against incipient wars cannot be carried out on a merely superficial level, by treating the symptoms. It must be done in a radical way, by attacking the causes. The reason I have called attention to the dimensions constituted by spiritual realities is my conern for the cause of peace, peace which is built up by men and women uniting around what is most fully and profoundly human, around what raises them above the world about them and determines their indestructible grandeur—indestructible in spite of the death to which everyone on earth is subject. I would like to add that the Catholic Church and, I think I can say, the whole of Christianity sees in this very domain its own particular task. The Second Vatican Council helped to establish what the Christian faith has in common with the various non-Christian religions in this aspiration. The Church is therefore grateful to all who show respect and good will with regard to this mission of hers and do not impede it or make it difficult. An anlysis of the history of mankind, especially at its present stage, shows how important is the duty of revealing more fully the range of the goods that are linked with the spiritual dimension of human existence. It shows how important this task is for building peace and how serious is any threat to human rights. Any violation of them, even in a "peace situation," is a form of warfare against humanity.

It seems that in the modern world there are two main threats. Both concern human rights in the field of international relations and human rights within the individual States or societies.

17. The first of these systematic threats against human rights is linked in an overall sense with the distribution of material goods. This distribution is frequently unjust both within individual societies and on the plan-

et as a whole. Everyone knows that these goods are given to man not only as nature's bounty: they are enjoyed by him chiefly as the fruit of his many activities, ranging from the simplest manual and physical labour to the most complicated forms of industrial production, and to the highly qualified and specialized research and study. Various forms of inequality in the possession of material goods, and in the enjoyment of them, can often be explained by different historical and cultural causes and circumstances. But, while these circumstances can diminish the moral responsibility of people today, they do not prevent the situations of inequality from being marked by injustice and social injury.

People must become aware that economic tensions within countries and in the relationship between States and even between entire continents contain within themselves substantial elements that restrict or violate human rights. Such elements are the exploitation of labour and many other abuses that affect the dignity of the human person. It follows that the fundamental criterion for comparing social, economic and political systems is not, and cannot be, the criterion of hegemony and imperialism: it can be, and indeed it must be, the humanistic criterion, namely the measure in which each system is really capable of reducing, restraining and eliminating as far as possible the various forms of exploitation of man and of ensuring for him, through work, not only the just distribution of the indispensable material goods, but also a participation, in keeping with his dignity, in the whole process of production and in the social life that grows up around that process. Let us not forget that, although man depends on the resources of the material world for his life, he cannot be their slave, but he must be their master. The words of the book of Genesis, "Fill the earth and subdue it" (*Gen.* 1:28), are in a sense a primary and essential directive in the field of economy and of labour policy.

18. Humanity as a whole, and the individual nations, have certainly made remarkable progress in this field during the last hundred years. But it is a field in which there is never any lack of systematic threats and violations of human rights. Disturbing factors are frequently present in the form of the frightful disparities between excessively rich individuals and groups on the one hand, and on the other hand the majority made up of the poor or indeed of the destitute, who lack food and opportunities for work and education and are in great numbers condemned to hunger and disease. And concern is also caused at times by the radical separation of work from property, by man's indifference to the production enterprise to which he is linked only by a work obligation, without feeling that he is working for a good that will be his or for himself.

It is no secret that the abyss separating the minority of the excessively rich from the multitude of the destitute is a very grave symptom in the life of any society. This must also be said with even greater insistence with regard to the abyss separating countries and regions of the earth. Surely the only way to overcome this serious disparity between areas of satiety and areas of hunger and depression is through coordinated cooperation by all countries. This requires above all else a unity inspired by an authentic perspective of peace. Everything will depend on whether these differences and contrasts in the sphere of the "possession" of goods will be systematically reduced through truly effective means, on whether the belts of hunger, malnutrition, destitution, underdevelopment, disease and illiteracy will disappear from the economic map of the earth, and on whether peaceful cooperation will avoid imposing conditions of exploitation and economic or political dependence, which would only be a form of neocolonialism.

19. I would now like to draw attention to a second systematic threat to man in his inalienable rights in the modern world, a threat which constitutes no less a danger than the first to the cause of peace. I refer to the various forms of injustice in the field of the spirit.

Man can indeed be wounded in his inner relationship with truth, in his conscience, in his most personal belief, in his view of the world, in his religious faith, and in the sphere of what are known as civil liberties. Decisive for these last is equality of rights without discrimination on grounds of origin, race, sex, nationality, religion, political convictions and the like. Equality of rights means the exclusion of the various forms of privilege for some and discrimination against others, whether they are people born in the same country or people from different backgrounds of history, nationality, race and ideology. For centuries the thrust of civilization has been in one direction: that of giving the life of individual political societies a form in which there can be fully safeguarded the objective rights of the spirit, of human conscience and of human creativity, including man's relationship with God. Yet in spite of this we still see in this field recurring threats and violations, often with no possibility of appealing to a higher authority or of obtaining an effective remedy.

Besides the acceptance of legal formulas safeguarding the principle of the freedom of the human spirit, such as freedom of thought and expression, religious freedom, and freedom of conscience, structures of social life often exist in which the practical exercise of these freedoms condemns man, in fact if not formally, to become a second-class or third-class citizen, to see compromised his chances of social advancement, his professional career or his access to certain posts of responsibility, and to lose even the possibility of educating his children freely. It is a question of the highest importance that in internal social life, as well as in international life, all human beings in every nation and country should be able to enjoy effectively their full rights under any political regime or system.

Only the safeguarding of this real completeness of rights for every human being without discrimination can ensure peace at its very roots.

20. With regard to religious freedom, which I, as Pope, am bound to have particularly at heart, precisely with a view to safeguarding peace, I would like to repeat here, as a contribution to respect for man's spiritual dimension, some principles contained in the Second Vatican Council's Declaration *Dignitatis Humanae:* "In accordance with their dignity, all human beings, because they are persons, that is, beings endowed with reason and free will and therefore bearing personal responsibility, are both impelled by their nature and bound by a moral obligation to seek the truth, especially religious truth. They are also bound to adhere to the truth once they come to know it and to direct their whole lives in accordance with its demands" *(Dignitatis Humanae,* 2).

"The practice of religion of its very nature consists primarily of those voluntary and free internal acts by which a human being directly sets his course towards God. No merely human power can either command or prohibit acts of this kind. But man's social nature itself requires that he give external expression to his internal acts of religion, that he communicate with others in religious matters and that he profess his religion in community" *(Dignitatis Humanae,* 3).

These words touch the very substance of the question. They also show how even the confrontation between the religious view of the world and the agnostic or even atheistic view, which is one of the "signs of the times" of the present age, could preserve honest and respectful human dimensions without violating the essential rights of conscience of any man or woman living on earth.

Respect for the dignity of the human person would seem to demand that, when the exact tenor of the exercise of religious freedom is being discussed or determined with a view to national laws or international conventions, the institutions that are by their nature at the service of religion should also be brought in. If this participation is omitted, there is a danger of imposing, in so intimate a field of man's life, rules or restrictions that are opposed to his true religious needs.

21. The United Nations Organization has proclaimed 1979 the Year of the Child. In the presence of the representatives of so many nations of the world gathered here, I wish to express the joy that we all find in children, the springtime of life, the anticipation of the future history of each of our present earthly homelands. No country on earth, no political system can think of its own future otherwise than through the image of these new generations that will receive from their parents the manifold

heritage of values, duties and aspirations of the nation to which they belong and of the whole human family. Concern for the child, even before birth, from the first moment of conception and then throughout the years of infancy and youth, is the primary and fundamental test of the relationship of one human being to another.

And so, what better wish can I express for every nation and the whole of mankind, and for all the children of the world than a better future in which respect for human rights will become a complete reality throughout the third millennium, which is drawing near.

22. But in this perspective we must ask ourselves whether there will continue to accumulate over the heads of this new generation of children the threat of common extermination for which the means are in the hands of the modern States, especially the major world powers. Are the children to receive the arms race from us as a necessary inheritance? How are we to explain this unbridled race?

The ancients said: *Si vis pacem, para bellum.* But can our age still really believe that the breathtaking spiral of armaments is at the service of world peace? In alleging the threat of a potential enemy, is it really not rather the intention to keep for oneself a means of threat, in order to get the upper hand with the aid of one's own arsenal of destruction? Here too it is the human dimension of peace that tends to vanish in favour of ever new possible forms of imperialism.

It must be our solemn wish here for our children, for the children of all the nations on earth, that this point will never be reached. And for that reason I do not cease to pray to God each day so that in his mercy he may save us from so terrible a day.

23. At the close of this address, I wish to express once more before all the high representatives of the States who are present a word of esteem and deep love for all the peoples, all the nations of the earth, for all human communities. Each one has its own history and culture. I hope that they will live and grow in the freedom and truth of their own history. For that is the measure of the common good of each one of them. I hope that each person will live and grow strong with the moral force of the community that forms its members as citizens. I hope that the State authorities, while respecting the just rights of each citizen, will enjoy the confidence of all for the common good. I hope that all the nations, even the smallest, even those that do not yet enjoy full sovereignty, and those that have been forcibly robbed of it, will meet in full equality with the others in the United Nations Organization. I hope that the United Nations will ever remain the supreme forum of peace and justice, the authentic seat of freedom of peoples and individuals in their longing for a better future.

The Role of the Laity

The last religious celebration of the Pope during his pilgrimage to Ireland was a Mass at Greenpark Racecourse, Limerick, on October 1, 1979. An estimated 250,000 people were present. After the Gospel, the Holy Father delivered the following homily:

1. On this last day of my visit to Ireland I come to you to celebrate with you the Holy Eucharist. I wish to seal once more, in the love of Christ Jesus, the bond that links the Successor of Peter in the See of Rome with the Church that is in Ireland. In you I greet once more all the People of Ireland, who have taken their place in the mystery of the Church through the preaching of Saint Patrick and through the Sacraments of Baptism and Confirmation. I invite you to make this last Mass, which I offer with you and for you, into a special hymn of thanksgiving to the most Holy Trinity for the days that I have been able to spend in your midst.

I come in the name of Christ to preach to you his own message. The liturgy of the word today speaks of a building, of the cornerstone that supports and gives strength to the house, of the city that is built on the hill for security and protection. These images contain an invitation for all of us, for all Christians, to come close to Christ, the cornerstone, so that he may become our support and the unifying principle which gives meaning and coherence to our lives. It is the same Christ who gives dignity to all the members of the Church and who assigns to each one his mission.

2. Today, I would like to speak to you about that special dignity and mission entrusted to the lay people in the Church. Saint Peter says that Christians are "a royal priesthood, a holy nation" (1 *Pt.* 2:9). All Christians, incorporated into Christ and his Church by baptism, are consecrated to God. They are called to profess the faith which they have received. By the sacrament of Confirmation, they are further endowed by the Holy Spirit with special strength to be witnesses of Christ and sharers in his mission of salvation. Every lay Christian is therefore an extraordinary work of God's grace and is called to the heights of holiness. Sometimes, lay men and women do not seem to appreciate to the full the dignity and the vocation that is theirs as lay people. No, there is no such thing as an "ordinary layman," for all of you have been called to conversion through the death and Resurrection of Jesus Christ. As God's holy people you are

called to fulfill your role in the evangelization of the world.

Yes, the laity are "a chosen race, a holy priesthood," also called to be "the salt of the earth" and "the light of the world." It is their specific vocation and mission to express the Gospel in their lives and thereby to insert the Gospel as a leaven into the reality of the world in which they live and work. The great forces which shape the world—politics, the mass media, science, technology, culture, education, industry and work—are precisely the areas where lay people are especially competent to execute their mission. If these forces are guided by people who are true disciples of Christ, and who are, at the same time, fully competent in the relevant secular knowledge and skill, then indeed will the world be transformed from within by Christ's redeeming power.

3. Lay people today are called to a strong Christian commitment: to permeate society with the leaven of the Gospel, for Ireland is at a point of decision in her history. The Irish people have to choose today their way forward. Will it be the transformation of all strata of humanity into a new creation, or the way that many nations have gone, giving excessive importance to economic growth and material possessions while neglecting the things of the spirit? The way of substituting a new ethic of temporal enjoyment for the law of God? The way of false freedom which is only slavery to decadence? Will it be the way of subjugating the dignity of the human person to the totalitarian domination of the State? The way of violent struggle between classes? The way of extolling revolution over God?

Ireland must choose. You the present generation of Irish people must decide; your choice must be clear and your decision firm. Let the voice of your forefathers, who suffered so much to maintain their faith in Christ and thus to preserve Ireland's soul, resound today in your ears through the voice of the Pope when he repeats the words of Christ: "What will it profit a man, if he gains the whole world, and forfeits his life?" (*Mt.* 16:26). What would it profit Ireland to go the easy way of the world and suffer the loss of her own soul?

Your country seems in a sense to be living again the temptations of Christ: Ireland is being asked to prefer the "kingdoms of the world and their splendour" to the Kingdom of God (cf. *Mt.* 4:8). Satan, the Tempter, the Adversary of Christ, will use all his might and all his deceptions to win Ireland for the way of the world. What a victory he would gain, what a blow he would inflict on the Body of Christ in the world, if he could seduce Irish men and women away from Christ. Now is the time of testing for Ireland. This generation is once more a generation of decision.

Dear sons and daughters of Ireland, pray, pray not to be led into temptation. I asked in my first Encyclical for a "great, intense and growing prayer for all the Church." I ask you today for a great, intense and growing prayer for all the people of Ireland, for the Church in Ireland, for all the Church which owes so much to Ireland. Pray that Ireland may not fail in the test. Pray as Jesus taught us to pray: "Lead us not into temptation, but deliver us from evil."

Above all, have an immense confidence in the merits of our Lord Jesus Christ and in the power of his death and Resurrection. It is precisely because of the strength of his Paschal Mystery that each of us and all Ireland can say: "I can do all things in him who strengthens me" (*Phil.* 4:13).

4. Ireland in the past displayed a remarkable interpenetration of her whole culture, speech and way of life by the things of God and the life of grace. Life was in a sense organized around religious events. The task of this generation of Irish men and women is to transform the more complex world of modern industry and urban life by the same Gospel spirit. Today, you must keep the city and the factory for God, as you have always kept the farm and the village community for him in the past. Material progress has in so many places led to decline of faith and growth in Christ, growth in love and in justice.

To accomplish this you must have, as I said in Phoenix Park, consistency between your faith and your daily life. You cannot be a genuine Christian on Sunday, unless you try to be true to Christ's spirit also in your work, your commercial dealings, at your trade union or your employers' or professional meetings. How can you be a true community in Christ at Mass unless you try to think of the welfare of the whole national community when decisions are being taken by your particular sector or group? How can you be ready to meet Christ in judgment unless you remember how the poor are affected by the behaviour of your group or by your personal life style? For Christ will say to us all: "In so far as you did this to one of the least of these brothers of mine, you did it to me" (*Mt.* 25:40).

I have learned with great joy and gratitude of the wonderful spirit of work and cooperation with which you all joined in the material preparations as well as the spiritual preparation for my visit. How much more wonderful still it would be if you could have the same spirit of work and cooperation always "for the glory of God and the honour of Ireland"!

5. Here in Limerick, I am in a largely rural area and many of you are people of the land. I feel at home with you as I did with the rural and mountain people of my native Poland, and I repeat here to you what I told them: Love the land; love the work of the fields for it keeps you close to God, the Creator, in a special way.

To those who have gone to the cities, here or abroad, I say: Keep in contact with your roots in the soil of Ireland, with your families and your culture. Keep true to the faith, to the prayers and the values you learned here; and pass on that heritage to your children, for it is rich and good.

To all I say, revere and protect your family and your family life, for the family is the primary field of Christian action for the Irish laity, the place where your "royal priesthood" is chiefly exercised. The Christian family has been in the past Ireland's greatest spiritual resource. Modern conditions and social changes have created new patterns and new difficulties for family life and for Christian marriage. I want to say to you: do not be discouraged, do not follow the trends where a close-knit family is seen as outdated; the Christian family is more important for the Church and for society today than ever before.

It is true that the stability and sanctity of marriage are being threatened by new ideas and by the aspirations of some. Divorce, for whatever reason it is introduced, inevitably becomes easier and easier to obtain and it gradually comes to be accepted as a normal part of life. The very possibility of divorce in the sphere of civil law makes stable and permanent marriages more difficult for everyone. May Ireland always continue to give witness before the modern world to her traditional commitment to the sanctity and the indissolubility of the marriage bond. May the Irish always support marriage, through personal commitment and through positive social and legal action.

Above all, hold high the esteem for the wonderful dignity and grace of the Sacrament of marriage. Prepare earnestly for it. Believe in the spiritual power which this Sacrament of Jesus Christ gives to strengthen the marriage union, and to overcome all the crises and problems of life together. Married people must believe in the power of the Sacrament to make them holy; they must believe in their vocation to witness through their marriage to the power of Christ's love. True love and the grace of God can never let marriage become a self-centred relationship of two individuals, living side by side for their own interests.

6. And here, I want to say a very special word to all Irish parents. Marriage must include openness to the gift of children. Generous openness to accept children from God as the gift to their love is the mark of the Christian couple. Respect the God-given cycle of life, for this respect is part of our respect for God himself, who created male and female, who created them in his own image, reflecting his own life-giving love in the patterns of their sexual being.

And so I say to all, have an absolute and holy respect for the sacredness of human life from the first moment of its conception. Abortion, as the Vatican Council stated, is one of the "abominable crimes" (*Gaudium et Spes,* 51). To attack unborn life at any moment from its conception is to undermine the whole moral order which is the true guardian of the wellbeing of man. The defence of the absolute inviolability of unborn life is part of the defence of human rights and human dignity. May Ireland never weaken in her witness, before Europe and before the whole world, to the dignity and sacredness of all human life, from conception until death.

Dear fathers and mothers of Ireland, believe in your vocation, that beautiful vocation of marriage and parenthood which God has given to you. Believe that God is with you—for all parenthood in heaven and on earth takes its name from him. Do not think that anything you will do in life is more important than to be a good Christian father and mother. May Irish mothers, young women and girls not listen to those who tell them that working at a secular job, succeeding in a secular profession, is more important than the vocation of giving life and caring for this life as a mother. The future of the Church, the future of humanity depend in great part on parents and on the family life that they build in their homes. The family is the true measure of the greatness of a nation, just as the dignity of man is the true measure of civilization.

7. Your homes should always remain homes of prayer. As I leave today this island which is so dear to my heart, this land and its people which is such a consolation and strength to the Pope, may I express a wish: that every home in Ireland may remain, or may begin again to be, a home of daily family prayer. That you would promise me to do this would be the greatest gift you could give me as I leave your hospitable shores.

I know that your Bishops are preparing a pastoral programme designed to encourage greater sharing by parents in the religious education of their children under the motto "handing on the faith in the home." I am confident that you will all join in this programme with enthusiasm and generosity. To hand on to your children the faith you received from your parents is your first duty and your greatest privilege as parents. The home should be the first school of religion, as it must be the first school of prayer. The great spiritual influence of Ireland in the history of the world was due in great degree to the religion of the homes of Ireland, for here is where evangelization begins, here is where vocations are nurtured. I appeal therefore to Irish parents to continue fostering vocations to the priesthood and the religious life in their homes, among their sons and daughters. It was, for generations, the greatest desire of every Irish parent to have a son a priest or religious, to have a daughter consecrated to God. May it continue to be your desire and your prayer. May increased opportunities for boys and girls never lessen your esteem for the privilege of having a son or daughter of yours selected by Christ and called by him to give up all things and follow him.

I entrust all this to Mary, bright "Sun of the Irish race." May her prayers help all Irish homes to be like the holy house of Nazareth. From them may young Christians go forth, as Jesus did from Nazareth. May they go forth in the power of the Spirit to continue Christ's work and to follow in his footsteps towards the end of the millennium, into the twenty-first century. Mary will keep you all close to him, who is "Father of the world to come" (*Is.* 9:6).

Dia agus Muire libh!

May God and Mary be with you and with the families of Ireland, always!

Religious Freedom a Right

Message of Pope John Paul II
to the Secretary-General
of the United Nations Organization
(December 2, 1978)

To His Excellency Dr. Kurt Waldheim, secretary-general of the United Nations Organization.

The signal occasion of the 30th anniversary of the Universal Declaration of Human Rights gives the Holy See the opportunity of proclaiming once again to people and to nations its constant interest and solicitude for the fundamental human rights whose expression we find clearly taught in the gospel message itself.

With this in mind I want to greet you, Mr. Secretary-General, and through you the president and members of the general assembly of the United Nations who have gathered to commemorate this anniversary. I want to express to all of you my firm agreement to "the continuing commitment of the United Nations Organization to promote in an ever clearer, more authoritative and more effective manner, respect for the fundamental rights of man" (Pope Paul VI, *Message for the XXVth Anniversary of the Declaration of Human Rights,* December 10, 1973: *AAS* 65 (1973) 674).

In these past 30 years significant steps have been taken and some outstanding efforts made to create and support the juridical instruments which would protect the ideals set out in this declaration.

Two years ago the International Covenant on Economic, Social and Cultural Rights and the International Covenant on Civil and Political Rights came into effect. By them, the United Nations marked a significant step forward in making effective one of the basic principles which it has adopted as its own from the very foundation of the organization: namely, to establish juridically binding means for promoting the human rights of individuals and for protecting their fundamental liberties.

Certainly, it would be a desirable goal to have more and more states adopt these covenants in order that the content of the universal declaration can become ever more operative in the world. In this way the declaration would find greater echo as the expression of the firm will of people everywhere to promote by legal safeguards the rights of all men and women without discrimination of race, sex, language or religion.

It should be noted that the Holy See—consistent with its own identity and at various levels—has always sought to be a faithful collaborator with the United Nations in all those initiatives which would further this noble but difficult task. The Holy See has always appreciated, lauded and supported the efforts of the United Nations endeavoring to guarantee in an ever more efficient way the full and just protection of the basic rights and freedoms of the human person.

If a review of the past 30 years gives us all reason for real satisfaction at the many advances which have been made in this field, still we cannot ignore that the world we live in today offers too many examples of situations of injustice and oppression. One is bound to observe a seemingly growing divergence between the meaningful declarations of the United Nations and the sometimes massive increase of human rights violations in all parts of society and of the world. This can only sadden us and leave us dissatisfied at the current state of affairs.

Who can deny that today individual persons and civil powers violate basic rights of the human person with impunity: rights such as the right to be born, the right to life, the right to responsible procreation, to work, to peace, to freedom and social justice, the right to participate in the decisions that affect people and nations?

And what can be said when we face the various forms of collective violence like racial discrimination against individuals and groups, the use of physical and psychological torture perpetrated against prisoners or political dissenters? The list grows when we turn to the instances of the sequestration of persons for political reasons and look at the acts of kidnapping for material gain which so dramatically attack family life and the social fabric.

In the world as we find it today what criteria can we use to see that the rights of all persons are protected? What basis can we offer as the soil in which individual and social rights might grow?

Unquestionably, that basis is the dignity of the human person.

Pope John XXIII explained this in *Pacem in Terris:* "Any well-regulated and profitable association of men in society demands the acceptance of one fundamental principle: that each individual is truly a person.

"As such he has rights and duties which together flow as a direct consequence from his nature. These rights and duties are universal and inviolable and therefore altogether inalienable" (Pope John XXIII, Encyclical Letter *Pacem in Terris* (April 11, 1963), no. 9).

Quite similar is the preamble of the universal declaration itself when it says: "The recognition of the inherent dignity and of the equal and inalienable rights of all members of the human family is the foundation of freedom, justice and peace in the world."

It is in this dignity of the person that human rights find their immediate source and it is respect for this dignity that gives birth to their effective protection. The human person, even when he or she errs, always maintains inherent dignity and never forfeits his or her personal dignity (see *Pacem in Terris,* no. 158).

For believers, it is by allowing God to speak to man that one can contribute more truly to the strengthening of the consciousness that every human being has of his or her destiny, and to the awareness that all rights derive from the dignity of the person who is firmly rooted in God.

I wish now to speak of these rights themselves as sanctioned by the declaration and, especially, of one of them which undoubtedly occupies a central position: the right to freedom of thought, of conscience and of religion (cf. Article 18).

Allow me to call the attention of the assembly to the importance and the gravity of a problem still today very keenly felt and suffered. I mean the problem of religious freedom, which is at the basis of all other freedoms and is inseparably tied to them all by reason of that very dignity which is the human person.

True freedom is the salient characteristic of humanity: it is the fount from which human dignity flows; it is "the exceptional sign of the divine image within man" (Vatican II, *Pastoral Constitution on the Church in the World of Today,* no. 17). It is offered to us and conferred on us as our own mission.

Today men and women have an increased consciousness of the social dimension of life and, as a result, have become ever more sensitive to the principle of freedom of thought, of conscience and of religion. However, with sadness and deeply felt regret we also have to admit that unfortunately, in the words of the Second Vatican Council, in its Declaration on Religious Freedom, "forms of government still exist under which, even though freedom of religious worship receives constitutional recognition, the powers of government are engaged in the effort to deter citizens from the profession of religion and to make life difficult and dangerous for religious communities" (Vatican II, *Declaration on Religious Freedom,* no. 15).

The Church strives to be the interpreter of the thirst modern men and women have for dignity. So I would solemnly ask that, in every place and by everyone, religious freedom be respected for every person and for all peoples. I am moved to make this solemn appeal because of the profound conviction that, even aside from the desire to serve God, the common good of society itself "may profit by the moral qualities of justice and peace which have their origin in man's faithfulness to God and to His holy will" (*Declaration on Religious Freedom,* no. 6). The free exercise of religion benefits both individuals and governments. Therefore the obligation to respect religious freedom falls on everyone, both private citizens and legitimate civil authority.

Why then is repressive and discriminatory action practiced against vast numbers of citizens, who have had to suffer all sorts of oppression, even death, simply in order to preserve their spiritual values, yet who, despite all this, have never ceased to cooperate in everything that serves the true civil and social progress of their country? Should they not be the objects of admiration and praise rather than considered as suspect and criminals?

My predecessor Paul VI raised this question: "Can a state fruitfully call for entire trust and collaboration while, by a kind of 'negative confessionalism,' it proclaims itself atheist and while declaring that it respects within a certain framework individual beliefs takes up positions against the faith of part of its citizens?" (Pope Paul VI, Address to the Diplomatic Corps (January 14, 1978): *AAS* 70 (1978) 170).

Justice, wisdom and realism all demand that the baneful positions of secularism be overcome, particularly the erroneous reduction of the religious fact to the purely private sphere. Every person must be given the opportunity within the context of our life together to profess his or her faith and belief, alone or with others in private and in public.

There is one last point which deserves attention. While insisting—and rightly so—on the vindication of human rights, every individual has the obligation to exercise his basic rights in a responsible and ethically justified manner. Every man and woman has the duty to respect in others the rights claimed for oneself. Furthermore, we must all contribute our share to the building up of a society that makes possible and feasible the enjoyment of rights and the discharge of the duties inherent in those rights.

To conclude this message, I wish to extend to you, Mr. Secretary-General, and to all those who, in whatever capacity, serve in your organization, my heartfelt good wishes, with the hope that the United Nations will continue tirelessly to promote everywhere the defense of the human person and of his dignity in the spirit of the universal declaration.

From the Vatican, December 2, 1978.

John Paul II, Pope

Trials of the Elderly With Christ at the Cross

Discourse of Pope John Paul II
to an Audience of Senior Citizens in Munich
(November 19, 1980)

Dear brothers and sisters who are advanced in age, it fills me with special joy that during my visit to Germany I am able to meet with you in a special hour of prayer.

I come as to familiar friends, for I know that in my service I am supported in a special way by your concern, prayer and sacrifice. So I greet you here in the Cathedral of Our Lady in Munich with heartfelt gratitude.

I especially thank you for the profound words of welcome and for the prayers with which you accompanied me during these days. Together with you I greet all the people of your age group in your country, especially those who are united with us through radio and television in this moment.

"Gruss Gott" (God greet you) to all of you who longer than myself have "endured the work and heat of the day" (*Mt.* 20:12), who have sought to meet the Lord longer than myself and to serve Him in all fidelity, in the great things and in the small ones, in joy and in suffering.

1. The pope bows with reverence before old age and he invites all people to do the same with him. Old age is the crown of the steps of life. It gathers in the harvest, the harvest of what you have learned and experienced, the harvest of what you have done and achieved, the harvest of what you have suffered and undergone.

As in the finale of a great symphony, all the themes of life combine to a mighty harmony. And this harmony bestows wisdom—the wisdom which meant more to him than power and riches, more than beauty and health (see *Wis.* 7:7, 8, 10), the wisdom of which we read in the rules of life of the Old Testament (how fine a thing, wisdom in the aged) and considered advice coming from men of distinction. The crown of the old is ripe experience, their true glory, fear of the Lord (*Sir.* 25:5 ff.).

To today's older generation, that is to you, my dear brothers and sisters, this crown of wisdom is due in a very special way: some of you had, in two world wars, seen and endured immense pain; many of you lost relatives, health, profession, house and home. You have come to know the abyss of the human heart, but also its capacity for heroic willingness to help and loyalty to the faith, as well as its power to dare make a new beginning.

Wisdom confers distance, but not a distance which stands aloof from the world. It allows people to be above things without despising them, it allows us to see the world with the eyes—and with the heart—of God. It allows us, with God, to say "yes" even to our limitations, even to our past—with its disappointments, omissions and sins.

For "we know that God turns everything to the good for all who love him" (*Ps.* 8:28). From the conciliatory power of this wisdom spring kindness, patience, understanding and—that precious ornament of age—a sense of humor.

You yourselves know best, my dear sisters and brothers, that this precious harvest of life which the Creator has apportioned to you is not an uncontested possession.

It requires vigilance, carefulness, self-control and sometimes even resolute battle. Otherwise it is easily in danger of being eaten away or corroded by idleness, by moods, by superficiality, by arrogance or even by bitterness.

Do not lose heart. With the grace of our Lord begin over and over again and use the sources of power which he offers you: in the sacrament of the bread and of forgiveness, in the world which comes to you in sermons and in reading and in spiritual conversation.

In this place I am sure that I may also in your name most cordially thank the priests who reserve a decisive place in their work and in their hearts for pastoral work among the aged. In this way they at the same time render the best service to their whole community, for they win, in a sense, a legion of faithful intercessors for it.

After the priests who serve you with their pastoral work, I should like to address myself to the priests of your age group. My dear brothers, the Church thanks you for your lifelong work in the vineyard of the Lord.

To younger priests Jesus says in the Gospel of John: "Others have worked, and you have come into the rewards of their trouble" (*Jn.* 14:28). Most venerable presbyters, keep on bringing the needs of the Church before God through your priestly service of prayer—*"ad deum, qui laetificat iuventutem vestram"* (*Ps.* 43:4).

2. Brothers and sisters of the older generation, you are a treasure for the Church, you are a blessing to the world. How often you have to relieve young parents, how well you know how to introduce the youngsters to the history of our family and your homeland, the tales of your people and the world of faith.

The young with problems often find an easier way to you than to the generation of their parents. To your sons and daughters you are the most precious support in their hours of difficulty. With your advice and your commitment, you cooperate in many committees, associations and initiatives in church and public life.

You are a necessary complement in a world which shows enthusiasm for the vitality of youth and for the power of the so-called "best years," in a world where what can be counted counts so much.

You remind it that it is building upon the diligence of those who were young and strong earlier, and that one day it, too, will pass its work along in turn, into even younger hands.

It becomes apparent in you that the meaning of life cannot consist of earning and spending money, that in all our external activities there has to mature something internal, and something eternal in the temporal, according to the word of St. Paul, "though this outer man of ours may be falling into decay, the inner man is renewed day by day" (*Cor.* 4:16).

Indeed, old age deserves our reverence, a reverence which shines forth from holy Scripture when it lets us see Abraham and Sarah, when it calls Simeon and Anna to the holy family in the temple, when it calls for priests "elders" (*Acts* 14:23; 15:7; *Tim.* 4:14; 5:17, 19; *Tit.* 1:5; *Pt.* 5:1), when it sums up the worship of the whole of creation in the adoration of the 24 elders, when finally God calls himself "the ancient of days."

3. Is it possible to sing a higher song in honor of the dignity of old age? But, my dear old hearers, I am sure you would be disappointed if the pope did not also mention another aspect of becoming old, if he only brought you the—maybe unexpected—honors, but failed to bring you solace.

To the beautiful season in which we stand not only belong the harvest and the solemn splendor of color, but also branches are being stripped of their leaves. The leaves fall and decay, there is not only the soft and full light, but also wet and dreary fog.

In the same way old age contains not only the final accord, a reconciled summing up of life, but also the time of fading, a time where the world becomes strange and life can turn into a burden and the body into pain. And so I add to my call "be aware of your dignity" the other one "accept your burden."

For most people the burden of old age means in the first place a certain frailty of the body. The senses are no longer as acute, the limbs no longer as pliable as they used to be, the organs become more sensitive (see *Sir.* 12:3 ff.). The things one may experience in younger years in days of sickness become often one's daily—and nightly—companions in old age. One is forced to give up many activities which used to be familiar and dear.

Also the memory may refuse its service: new information is no longer received easily, old knowledge fades away. And so the world ceases to be familiar—the world of the family, the living and working conditions of the adults utterly changes; the interests and forms of expression of young people are completely different; the children have new learning aims and methods.

The homeland becomes strange, with its growing cities, the increasing density of population, the landscape many times remodeled. The world of politics and economics is strange; the world of social and medical care becomes anonymous and unintelligible.

And even that domain where we should feel at home most of all—the Church in its life and doctrine—has become strange to many of you through her effort to meet the demands of the times and the expectations and needs of the younger generation.

You feel misunderstood and often rejected by this world which is hard to understand. Your opinion, your cooperation, your presence is not asked for—that is how you feel, and unfortunately, sometimes it is true.

4. What can the pope say to this? How shall I console you? I do not want to take it too easy. I do not want to belittle the anxieties of old age, your weaknesses and illnesses, your helplessness and loneliness. But I would like to see them in a reconciling light—in the light of our Savior "Who for us did sweat blood, Who for us was scourged at the pillar, Who for us was crowned with thorns."

In the trials of old age He is the companion of your pain, and you are His companions on His way of the cross. There is no tear you have to shed alone, and none you shed in vain (see *Ps.* 56:9).

By this suffering He has redeemed suffering, and through your suffering you cooperate in His salvation (see *Col.* 1:24). Accept your suffering as His embrace and turn it into a blessing by accepting it from the hand of the Father. In His inscrutable, yet unquestionable wisdom and love He is using this to bring about your perfection. It is in the furnace that ore turns into gold (see 1 *Pt.* 1:7); it is in the press that the grape becomes wine.

In this spirit—which God alone can give us—it becomes also easier to be understanding with those who, through negligence, carelessness, or heedlessness, add to our need, and it becomes possible for us to forgive also those who knowingly and even intentionally make us suffer without conceiving fully, however, how much pain they cause us.

"Father, forgive them, for they do not know what they are doing" (*Lk.* 23:34). Also with regard to us was this word, which alone brings salvation, spoken.

5. In this spirit—which we shall implore together and for each other

in this hour—we are also going to be gratefully awake to all loving thoughts, words and deeds which we receive each day, which we so easily get used to and which therefore we easily take for granted and which we overlook.

We are celebrating today the feast of St. Elizabeth, a saint your nation gave to the whole world as a symbol of self-sacrificing charity. She is the sublime example and patroness for all who serve their fellow creatures in need—be it through their profession or on an honorary basis, be it in the circle of their friends and relatives all who in them meet Christ—whether they know it or not.

That, my dear older people, is the reward which you give to those to whom you dislike to be a burden. You are the occasion for them to meet the Lord, the opportunity to outgrow themselves. By your turning to them you let them share in the already mentioned fruits of life which God allowed to ripen in you.

Therefore do not bury your requests in a timid, disappointed or reproachful heart, but express them in all naturalness—being convinced of your own dignity and of the good in the hearts of the others.

And be glad at each opportunity to practice that royal word of "Thank you" which rises from all altars and which will fill our eternal blessedness.

So I am sure that I may, with you, thank all those people who work for the well-being of the older generation, for their well-being in body and mind, in order to help them find a fulfilled life and a permanent home in society—all those who work in the many ecclesiastical, civil and public organizations, associations and initiatives, on a communal or on a higher level, in legislature and administration or just on a private basis.

I commend especially the fact that working for elderly people is becoming more and more working with elderly people.

6. With this I turn again to you, my elder brothers and sisters, and to the consolation you expect from me. There is a saying: "When you are lonely, go and visit somebody who is lonelier than you."

This wisdom I would like to recommend to you. Open your mind for those companions on your road who in whatever respect are in still poorer condition than you. You can help them in one way or the other—through conversation, through giving a hand, some favor or at least your manifest sympathy.

I promise you in the name of Jesus: in this you are going to find strength and consolation (see *Acts* 20:35). In this way, you experience in small matters what we all are in big ones. We are one body in many members—those who bring help and those who receive help, those who are healthy and those who are sick, those who are younger and those who are older: those who have stood the test of life, those who still are standing it, and those who just are growing into it; those who are young and those who once have been young; those who are old and those who are going to be old tomorrow.

We all together represent the fullness of the body of Christ, we all together mature into this fullness—"into the perfect man, fully ripe with the fullness of Christ" (*Eph.* 4:13).

7. The last consolation we are seeking together, my dear fellow pilgrims "in this vale of tears" (*Salve Regina*), is consolation in the face of death. Since our birth we have been going to meet it, but in old age we become more conscious of its approach from year to year—if only we do not drive it forcefully from our thoughts and feelings. The Creator has arranged it so that in old age accepting and standing the test of death is prepared for, made easier and learned in an almost natural manner. Hence becoming old, as we have seen, means a slow taking leave of the unbroken fullness of life, of unimpeded contact with the world.

The great school of living and dying then brings us to many an open grave; it makes us stand at many a deathbed before we are the ones around whom other people will be standing in prayer—so God grant.

An old person has experienced such lessons of life in greater number than the young do. He is seeing them with increasing frequency. That is his great advantage on the way to that great threshold which we often in a biased way conceive of as being an abyss of night.

The view across the threshold is dark from outside, but God in His love will allow those who have gone before us to accompany our lives and surround us with care more often than we may think.

The conviction of deep and living faith gave to a church in this city the name of "All Souls Church." The two German churches in Rome are called: "St. Mary of the Cemetery"—*"in Campo Santo"*—and "St. Mary of the Holy Souls"—*"Dell'anima."*

The more the fellow beings of our visible world reach the limits of their ability to help, the more we should see the messengers of the love of God in those who already have passed the test of death and who now wait for us over there: the saints, especially our personal patrons, and our deceased relatives and friends who we hope are at home in God's mercy.

Many of you, my dear sisters and brothers, have lost the visible presence of partners. To you I direct my pastoral admonition: allow God ever more to be the partner of your lives, then you will also be united to the one Whom he gave you as a companion once upon a time and Who now himself has found His center in God.

Without familiarity with God there is in the very end no consolation on earth. For that is exactly what God intends with death! That at least in this one sublime hour of our life we allow ourselves to fall into His love without any other security than just this love of His. How could we show Him our faith, our hopes, our love in a more lucid manner?

One last consideration in this context. I am sure it echoes the conviction of many a heart. Death itself is a consolation. Life on this earth, even if it were no "vale of tears," could not offer a home to us forever.

It would turn more and more into a prison, an "exile" (*Salve Regina*). "For all that passes is just a likeness: (Goethe, *Faust,* II, final chorus); and so the words of St. Augustine, which never lose their color, come to our lips: "You have created us for you, Lord, and our heart is restless until it rests in you" (*Confessions,* I, 1, 1).

And so there are not these who are destined to die and those who remain in so-called life. What is awaiting all of us is a birth, a transformation. We fear the pains with Jesus on the Mount of Olives, but its radiant end we already carry within ourselves, since at our baptism we have been submerged in the death and victory of Jesus (see *Rom.* 6:3, *Col.* 2:12).

Together with all of you, together with you here in Our Lady's cathedral, with you before radio and television, with all those whom I have been able to meet in these blessed days, with all the citizens and guests of this beautiful land, with all those who believe, and for all those who are seeking, with the children and young people, the adults and the old people, I would like in this hour of farewell to turn our meditation into prayer:

"You have been my protector from my mother's womb;
"Do not reject me now my strength is failing" (*Ps.* 71:6, 9).

"Come to our aid with Your mercy and keep us safe from temptation and sin, so that we may be full of confidence as we await the coming of our Savior Jesus Christ" (Order of the Mass).

And here in Our Lady's cathedral I would like to combine our prayer, which is always spoken in the spirit of Jesus and only through Jesus arrives at the Father, with the prayer of the one who, being the first to have been saved, is our mother and our sister (Paul VI, at the conclusion of the third session of the council, "Insegnamenti," II, pp. 675 and 664):

"Holy Mary, Mother of God,
Pray for us sinners
Now
And at the hour of our death, amen."

Amen. Praised be Jesus Christ.